Partnering with the Parents Of Today's College Students

Kurt Keppler, Richard H. Mullendore & Anna Carey,
Editors

NASPA
Student Affairs Administrators
in Higher Education

Additional copies may be purchased by contacting the NASPA publications department at 301-638-1749 or visiting http://www.naspa.org/publications.

ISBN 0-931654-35-1

Table of Contents

Contributors

Ms. Leslie A. Banahan is assistant vice president for student affairs at the University of Georgia (UGA). Before joining the staff at UGA, she worked at the University of Mississippi where she first designed and implemented orientation programs for international students and later developed and directed new orientation programs for all freshmen, transfer students, and parents. She continues to speak to hundreds of parents each summer during UGA orientation sessions and is the primary parent contact throughout the year for student concerns and problems.

Dr. Jeanette M. Barker is assistant professor at the University of Georgia in the Department of Counseling and Human Development Services and teaches in the College Student Affairs Administration program. She received her EdD from North Carolina State University in Higher Education Administration. Dr. Barker previously served as coordinator of student affairs assessment at Georgia State University.

Anna Carey is the director of New Student Services/Family Outreach at Western Washington University (WWU). Anna received a BA in Sociology from The University at Albany and an MA in College Student Personnel from Bowling Green State University. Her most recent work in enhancing services for family members at WWU has been establishing a parent volunteer group in collaboration with university advancement. She has worked with programs and services for the families of university students since 1990. Ms. Carey has held regional positions in the National Orientation Directors Association and NASPA.

Dr. Charlene M. Dukes is the vice president for student services at Prince George's Community College in Largo, Maryland where she has been on the staff for 9 years. She received her BS in English Education from Indiana University of Pennsylvania and her MEd and EdD from the University of Pittsburgh. She currently serves on the NASPA's Academy Board, Senior Student Affairs Officers

Institute, and the Health Education Leadership Program.

Dr. Bill Faulkner currently serves as the director of student leadership programs at the University of Central Florida where he has oversight over several student life areas. He earned a BA degree in Psychology from St. Andrews Presbyterian College in North Carolina and completed both his masters and doctorate degrees in Student Affairs Administration from the University of Georgia. He is a member of the core committee of the NASPA Student Leadership Programs Knowledge Committee that sponsors a variety of presentations and other professional development opportunities. More recently, he has had the opportunity to work with parents whose students are involved in a 2-year leadership development program.

Dr. Kimberly G. Frazier is a faculty instructor in the Department of University Studies at Kennesaw State University. Prior to her faculty appointment, Frazier served as director of new student programs at Georgia State University for 7 years. Frazier recently completed her doctorate in Educational Policy Studies at Georgia State University. Kim's research interests include student engagement and the first-year experience.

Sarah Honor is a graduate student currently seeking her masters degree in Student Affairs Administration at Western Washington University. She is currently supplementing her education with a position in the New Student Services office at Western focused on orientation, parent programs, and first-year programs. She also interns as an academic advisor at Skagit Valley College in Mount Vernon, Washington. She will graduate in August 2005.

Dr. Michael L. Jackson is vice president for student affairs at the University of Southern California. He earned his BA degree in Anthropology at Stanford University, and both his MEd and EdD from the

University of Massachusetts, Amherst. Prior to USC, he served as dean of students and assistant to the provost at Stanford University. He served as president of NASPA (2002-2003) and also served on their board of directors and as vice president of Region VI. He is a member of the board of trustees at the Robert Louis Stevenson School in Pebble Beach, CA. He also serves on accreditation teams for the Western Association for Senior Colleges and Universities (WASC) and the Middle States Commission. He currently serves as a member of the California Educational Facilities Authority.

Dr. Kurt Keppler is currently president of NASPA and serves as the vice president for student affairs at Valdosta State University. He previously served as associate vice president and dean of students at Georgia State University, associate dean of students at Virginia Commonwealth, and director of student development at the University of Missouri. He has served on the faculty at all four institutions. Keppler earned his doctoral and masters degrees from the University of Missouri and his bachelor's degree from the University of Wisconsin. Keppler was NASPA's Conference Chair for the 2003 national conference in St. Louis.

Dr. John Wesley Lowery is an assistant professor of higher education and student affairs at the University of South Carolina. He served as a member-at-large of the NASPA board of directors from 2002 to 2004 and is frequent presenter and author on legal and legislative issues in student affairs and higher education.

Dr. Richard H. Mullendore is a professor in the College Student Affairs Administration program at the University of Georgia. As a former chief student affairs officer at two state flagship universities, he has accumulated a wealth of experience in working with parents while simultaneously navigating the campus political environment. He has started parent programs at three institutions in collaboration with development offices, and is the coauthor of *Helping Your First-Year College Student Succeed: A Guide for Parents*. Mullendore is also a fellow of the National Resource Center for the First-Year Experience and Students in Transition

at the University of South Carolina. He has written and presented extensively on orientation and parent programs, and is a past president of the National Orientation Directors Association.

Sheila Murphy has served for the past 10 years as the dean for student life at Simmons College in Boston. She had previously served as the senior student affairs officer at Russell Sage College and Mount Holyoke College and has developed parent councils and increased programming for parents in each of these institutions. She has served NASPA as the national chair of the Women in Student Affairs Network (WISA) and as the regional vice president for Region I. She is the program chair for the 2005 NASPA Conference. She is a graduate of Stonehill College and the Harvard Graduate School of Education.

Dr. Karen L. Pennington was NASPA President 2003-2004 and has held seven mid- and senior-level student affairs positions within various types of institutions of higher education since 1980. In 1998 she became vice president of student development and campus life at Montclair State University in New Jersey. Prior to Montclair State, Dr. Pennington enjoyed a career in the State University of New York (SUNY) system, most recently as vice president for student and campus life at SUNY Geneseo, and dean for student life at SUNY New Paltz. Dr. Pennington received her PhD in Educational Administration from the University at Albany, her MA in History from the University of Scranton, her MEd in Counseling from Gannon University, and her BA in History from the University of Scranton. Dr. Pennington also serves as a member of the Board of Trustees of the University of Scranton.

Ms. Julie L. Ramsey is the vice president of college life and dean of students at Gettysburg College where she has been dean for over 14 years. She has established a parent e-newsletter at Gettysburg and has cochaired two NASPA conferences on spirituality in higher education. She is also the mother of a college-going freshman this fall.

Beth Saul is the director for parent programs and fraternity and sorority leadership development at the

University of Southern California (USC). She has been on the staff at USC for 16 years and established the Office for Parent Programs in 2002. The USC Office for Parent Programs was honored with the NASPA Region VI Innovative Program Award in November of 2003. Beth is a coauthor of *The Administration of Fraternal Organizations on North American Campuses: A Pattern for the New Millennium and Inspirations for Greeks* (College Administration Publications, 2004).

Dr. Renee Barnett Terry is the dean of student affairs at Revelle College (a distinctive undergraduate college system modeled after Oxford and Cambridge) at the University of California-San Diego. She has worked with parents of college students for the past 20 years and is particularly interested in millennial college students, underrepresented students, and the changing roles of parents of the millennials in higher education. Barnett Terry has been actively involved in the National Association of Student Personnel Administrators (NASPA), serving in a variety of roles including National Conference chair-Boston 2002, Region-VI Advisory Board member, NASPA Journal Board member, Western Regional Conference chair, Minority Undergraduate Fellows Program (MUFP) mentor, and other positions both regionally and nationally.

Dr. Craig Ullom has served in a variety of student affairs leadership positions at public and private colleges and universities over the last 29 years. He currently serves as associate vice president for campus life at the University of Central Florida and frequently conducts workshops and presentations nationally. Ullom earned his doctorate in Adult and Continuing Education from the University of Georgia and holds a master's degree in Counseling and Student Affairs from Eastern Illinois University. He is the founder and president of Collegiate Parents, Inc., that provides coaching and learning opportunities for parents of college-bound students.

Laura E. Valdez is the manager of new student orientation at the University of New Mexico in Albuquerque. She learned a lot about student/parent relationships when she developed and coordinated the Family Connection component, that runs concurrently with the student orientation program. She continues to work with parents in her current position in the dean of students office. Her bachelors and masters degrees are in Communication from the University of New Mexico. Laura has served on various NASPA initiatives at regional and national levels. She was recently appointed to serve on the NASPA MUFP advisory board.

Dr. Jeanine A. Ward-Roof is the director of student development services at Clemson University. She received her BS in Communication from Ohio University, MA in College Student Personnel from Bowling Green State University and a PhD in Educational Leadership from Clemson University. She has served as president of the National Orientation Directors Association and the South Carolina College Personnel Association. She has published on parent and orientation issues in a variety of venues including a monograph published jointly by the National Resource Center for the First-Year Experience and Students in Transition and the National Orientation Directors Association.

Andrew Wilson works as the assistant dean for campus life and director of student conduct at Emory University where oversees the campus judicial process and crisis management. Currently pursuing a PhD in Student Affairs Administration at the University of Georgia, he earned a master's degree from Virginia Tech's Higher Education in Student Affairs program and a bachelor's from Winthrop University. He has worked closely with students' families in his positions in residence life, judicial affairs, social justice education, and Greek affairs.

Foreword

Karen L. Pennington, NASPA President, 2003-2004

"Parents can only give [children] good advice or put them on their right paths,
but the final forming of a person lies in their own hands."

(Anne Frank, *Diary of a Young Girl*, date of entry July 15, 1944)

This sentiment is one to which many student affairs professionals would subscribe. But it is also one that often currently leads to a sense of frustration. The late 20th and early 21st centuries have brought with them a new sense of parenting and a need for higher education professionals to reevaluate and readjust the ways in which they work and relate to students.

Many students feel that they are adults; however parents often feel that their college-age student is little more than an older adolescent. For students whose educational journey supports a path of growth and development by the individual, any effort to delay that growth often feels like a hindrance and a nuisance.

But what are the reasons for the change in the way today's American parents seek to raise their children, and what does it mean for student affairs professionals and the concept of student development? Are parents partners in the educational process or are they obstacles to fostering growth and change? How can we balance our professional obligation to enhance student growth with the needs of parents who seek to be so involved in the day-to-day lives of their students? How can our role as educators, with the additional demands of today's society, be accomplished most effectively?

As educators, we are often at odds with parents in regards to students' actions on campus and how the college or university should respond. However, we both have the student's best interest at heart. Through partnerships with parents and families, we can create additional learning opportunities and also increase the likelihood of student success. But how do we come to a better understanding of our mutual desire to ensure student success? This book was commissioned to explore these and other questions about today's parents and our relationship to them and, therefore, to our students.

Educating ourselves for the new millennium is the first step toward redefining and restructuring our effectiveness as professionals. The information provided in this book will serve as an important part of this journey.

Preface

Kurt Keppler, Richard H. Mullendore, and Anna Carey

> We who are in the business of working with students must not lose sight of the influence of the family system. Although our primary relationships will always be with students, we diminish our potential to enhance their development if we discount the relationships that can be initiated with their families.
>
> (Austin, 2003, p. 146)

The parents of today's students interact with college staff and faculty much more frequently and for different reasons than parents of previous generations. Institutions must decide on the type of relationship they wish to have with parents; do they desire a partnership, an arms' length relationship, or something in between? While there is a plethora of research available on generational differences and today's college student, most of the information about parents is anecdotal and generally found in magazines and newspapers. This National Association of Student Personnel Administrators (NASPA) publication is written by student affairs practitioners who possess a wealth of knowledge about today's parents. The monograph addresses generational differences but is primarily focused on parents and family members of college students. Chapters will cover demographic perspectives, developmental issues, parent programming, problem solving, legal issues, best practices, and a literature review.

"Parents who understand how the institution functions, who meet and interact with resource people, and who are committed to developing effective communication patterns with their students can become institutional advocates and positive retention agents" (Mullendore, 1998, p. 58). As authors of this book, we hope the reader will realize the key role parents and families play in the success of college students. Our goal is to provide a complete and integrated approach to working with parents at your institution. Creating a structure that provides opportunities for parents to participate in the college experience can pay huge dividends in terms of increased student success,

institutional financial support, and enhanced public relations. As with so many aspects of our work, the opportunity for building bridges, creating awareness, and educating others about the dynamics that lead to student success is ours to develop.

It is important that we keep in mind the voice of today's parents, captured so succinctly in a commencement speech by Anna Quindlen, an author, former *New York Times* reporter, and parent of three children:

> But we are only human, and being a parent is a very difficult job, more difficult than any other, because it requires the shaping of other people, which is an act of extraordinary hubris. Over the years we learned to want for you things that you did not want for yourself. We learned to want the lead in the play, the acceptance to our own college, the straight and narrow path that often leads absolutely nowhere. Sometimes we wanted those things because we were convinced it would make life better, or at least easier for you. Sometimes we had a hard time distinguishing between where you ended and we began. (Quindlen, 1999, ¶ 16)

This monograph also opens the discussion of unexamined issues and questions related to parental involvement and challenges colleagues to consider parent relations an area poised for further examination and exploration. We hope that this monograph provides institutions with a series of challenges and opportunities for discussion and action and encourages the development of a successful relationship between parents and colleges.

Today, *parent* may mean many things. The traditional nuclear family is simply one of many family structures, as students may have a single parent, a guardian, a member of the extended family, or someone else as their primary support network. The authors may refer to parent, family member, or others interchangeably throughout the monograph to indicate the complexity of the family entity.

In chapter 1, Developing a Partnership With Today's College Parents, Richard Mullendore, Leslie Banahan, and Julie Ramsey provide a framework that will assist staff in working with today's parents. Topics include developing an institutional philosophy for interacting with parents, resolving concerns/problems raised by parents, navigating the campus political scene, and educating/training staff and faculty to interact with parents.

Renee Barnett Terry, Charlene Dukes, Laura Valdez, and Andrew Wilson help the reader develop an understanding of today's parents and students from a demographic perspective in chapter 2, Changing Demographics and Diversity in Higher Education. The authors discuss the diverse populations of students entering higher education, and the parent and family influence on the lives of these students.

Chapter 3, Understanding the New Relationship, focuses on college student development from adolescence to adulthood, and the parent/student issues involved during this time of transition and change. Craig Ullom and Bill Faulkner discuss how these issues affect the work of student affairs professionals.

In chapter 4, Parents Orientation: Begin With the End in Mind, Jeanine Ward-Roof provides extensive detail regarding what may be the college's best opportunity to acclimate parents to college life. Topics include developing a parent orientation program, current practices in parent orientation, and recommendations for those implementing or modifying a program for parents.

Richard Mullendore and Leslie Banahan offer strategies for the development and/or expansion of parent

programming efforts in chapter 5, Channeling Parent Energy and Reaping the Benefits. The authors discuss planning parent/family weekends; communicating with parents electronically or via hard copy; developing a parent programs office and a parent/family association; creating a parent advisory council; and cultivating parents for fund-raising opportunities.

Today's parents often want to know as much as possible about their student's college experience, including information that may be legally protected. In chapter 6, Legal Issues Regarding Partnering With Parents: Misunderstood Federal Laws and Potential Sources of Institutional Liability, John Wesley Lowery summarizes the myriad of legal issues pertaining to student information and student records.

Chapter 7, Managing Parent Expectations: My How Times have Changed, by Michael Jackson and Sheila Murphy, investigates the changing roles and attitudes of parents regarding involvement with their student's college experience. A historical perspective is provided along with an introduction to various college activities designed for parents and families.

The monograph concludes with an annotated bibliography and list of resources prepared by Jeanette Barker and Kimberly Frazier. Also, Appendix A contains model programs from various institutions, gathered by Beth Saul and Sarah Honor.

This publication is written primarily for student affairs professionals; however, others will also find valuable insight, and the book provides an abundance of information for anyone interested in understanding today's student/parent/college relationship. Parents and family members will learn about the nuances of this relationship and discover new avenues for improving communication and becoming better informed regarding campus policies, procedures, and involvement opportunities. Student affairs professionals will gain insight into the parent/student relationship and the reasons why today's parents may seem more intrusive. The monograph also provides tangible ideas for colleges to implement to serve parents and family members in ways that will enhance student success.

We are grateful for being given the opportunity to explore this timely topic, and appreciate the vision of Gwen Dungy and her staff in the NASPA central office for conceptualizing this project. We would be remiss if we didn't offer a special thank you to NASPA's director of publications, Jesse Ward, for keeping us on track throughout the process.

References

Austin, D. M. (2003). The role of family influence on student success. In J. A. Ward-Roof and C. Hatch (Eds.), *Designing successful transitions: A guide for orienting students to college* (Monograph No.13, 2nd ed.) (pp. 137-147). Columbia, SC: National Resource Center for The First-Year Experience and Students in Transition.

Mullendore, R. H. (1998). Including parents and families in the orientation process. In R. H. Mullendore (Ed.), *Orientation planning manual* (pp. 56-62). Bloomington, IN: National Orientation Directors Association.

Quindlen, A. (1999). Commencement speech. Retrieved January 14, 2005, from Mount Holyoke College, Office of Communications website, http://www.mtholyoke.edu/offices/comm/oped/Quindlen.shtml

Chapter 1
Developing a Partnership With Today's College Parents

Richard H. Mullendore, Leslie A. Banahan, and Julie L. Ramsey

At 6:30 a.m., the chief student affairs officer is awakened by the president of the college who has just received an angry telephone call from the CEO of one of the largest banks in the state. What is the issue? The banker's daughter has no hot water for her shower in the residence hall! The chief student affairs officer quickly informs the director of housing who contacts the head resident who calls the resident assistant on the floor. The resident assistant fills out a maintenance form and gives it to the clerk at the front desk, who calls the physical plant to fix the problem. Another day of meeting parents' expectations has begun.

It is no secret that today's generation of baby-boomer parents seeks to play a more expanded role in the lives and education of their sons and daughters. Whatever we, as student affairs professionals, may think about this change, it is happening, and we would do best to understand this change and use our creativity to adapt to it. Given other significant issues in the world of higher education—new demographics, new and expensive technology and increasing financial challenges facing many of our institutions—this change in parental expectations and behaviors may not seem all that momentous, but colleges that learn quickly how best to adjust to these new expectations will be doing themselves a significant service. Taking the lead to craft a successful institutional strategy for working with this important constituency is an essential part of the value that student affairs administrators can bring to their institutions.

As student affairs professionals, we will be most effective if we are able to proactively respond to the new expectations, assumptions, and mental models parents bring to higher education. Student affairs can be a motivating and facilitating force—we are on the front lines and are likely to see issues and potential solutions before others do—but we cannot act alone in shaping an institutional response. To accomplish this task, we must take into account a variety of institutional perspectives in order to craft a comprehensive philosophy of parent partnership.

As parents continue to increase their level of involvement, we have the opportunity to think differently about the way we work with them to build an effective alliance. How would our work be different if we accepted and welcomed this new generation of parents as partners in the educational process? Does our institution have a coherent and internally consistent message to parents about our expectations of them? What does partnering with the parents of today look like? What changes in our current practices does this entail for student affairs practitioners and our administrative and faculty colleagues?

Partnering may sound like a simple process; in reality, it is not. We should work from the premise that part of our job is educating parents about the role we believe we should play in their students' educational experiences. We can and should help them understand how they can best work with us to solve problems and create educational opportunities for their students. Partnership requires intentionality, clear goals, and well-developed institutional processes that create shared understandings. This chapter addresses the need for a clear institutional philosophy for partnering with parents, addresses key issues that emerge in the development of such a philosophy, and suggests a process to be used in the development of a philosophy of parent partnership.

Why Parents Intervene

As we think about our reactions to parental involvement, it may be useful to examine the reasons why parents are tempted to intervene. Why do parents attempt to intercede, or some would say, intrude, in their students' educational experiences? What assumptions underlie their need or desire to get involved? What are the forces at work in the parent/student relationship and in the world at large that are encouraging more and more of our parents to call the college first, rather than expect their students to secure information, solve problems, and advocate for themselves? One answer may be that some parents do not have full confidence in their student's ability to resolve issues independently. The fear of making a costly mistake is great. What are the repercussions for a student who fails to resolve a judicial complaint, a roommate dispute, or a financial disagreement with the business office? Although colleges and universities tend to be rather forgiving places, there are consequences associated with both actions and failure to act. Parents may intervene because they do not trust their students to advocate successfully, to document problems properly, to meet deadlines, or to perform other functions that organizational systems increasingly demand. When it comes to interacting with our institutions, many parents act on the principle, "If you want something done right, do it yourself." As the cost of going to college has risen, so has the sense that this investment is too important to risk it being sidetracked or undermined by a novice.

Other parents may intervene on their student's behalf out of guilt. With the busy lives so many parents lead and the greater distance that seeps into the parent/student relationship during college years, parents can easily feel detached or even alienated from their son or daughter. Out of regret and guilt, these parents are easily coaxed into the role of defender and savior of their student. Some parents may get involved because they think other parents are doing so, perceiving a disadvantage for their student if they fail to advocate for him/her.

Many of today's parents intervene because they presuppose that their involvement will change the situation, especially those situations over which administrators or faculty are assumed to have some control. Johnnie or Sally is not happy with a roommate assignment? Use your leverage! Call the dean, the president, or better yet, a trustee. Parents will often make subtle or not so subtle attempts at leverage; they hope by mentioning their status as full payers, legacies, or donors they can move things in a more favorable direction. They may be accustomed to getting their way in the business and professional world and are used to getting what they want through contacts, or even by threats and intimidation. They assume that the world of higher education works the same way and attempt to transfer these tactics from one context to the other.

Sometimes, parents are simply seeking information from us about how best to advise their son or daughter. They understand that they should not be attempting to insert themselves in the problem-solving role for their student. They recognize the temptation and are clear about the need to at least try to resist it. These parents often seek information to make sense of a situation which their student may have garbled, either intentionally or unintentionally. Some parents feel it is simply best to "go to the source," especially when the consequences of failure are significant and/or students are vague, unconcerned, confused, or overwhelmed by the situation facing them at college.

Our institutions may add to the confusion by sending mixed messages about the nature of higher education. Nearly all parents would accept the theoretical notion that significant learning occurs through trial and error, from making mistakes and learning to recognize and correct those mistakes. They recognize that in college their sons and daughters will be given rigorous assignments and will be expected to stretch, to learn in new ways, to learn to ask for help when they need it, and that learning can come of failure. This educational model, readily accepted in the classroom, is less often applied and supported outside the classroom. Parents who would never intrude in a dispute with a faculty member will readily pick up the telephone to contact a residence life coordinator or the dean of students. Relatively few parents are familiar with student development as a theoretical foundation for engaging with students. The little-understood and often poorly articulated student-development model is easily usurped by two other perspectives more common in the real world.

One perspective we encounter frequently is the customer service model. In this view, the educational experience is a commodity; money has been exchanged and satisfaction should be guaranteed. At private colleges, some parents paying the "full freight" have begun to distinguish themselves from those families who receive financial aid; they believe that since they are paying more tuition, they deserve better service.

Another perspective that is increasingly common is the legalistic model, focusing on the rights of students and parents. Of course, students and parents do have rights with regard to all of our institutions; however, parental interpretations and institutional interpretations of these same rights may vary greatly. Parents justifiably claim their students have the right to a safe living environment conducive to learning, but when the issue at hand is a dispute between two roommates in which both parties have some responsibility, the assertion of one's legal rights may obscure rather than illuminate an important learning opportunity for students. We often see a tendency for parents to invoke the threat of legal action against the university if their complaints are not resolved quickly and to their liking.

Considering all these possible motivations behind parents' desire to intervene can be helpful as we begin to craft an institutional approach to parents as partners. Depending on the situation, it is understandable that parents may be operating from a perspective or model different from that of the college staff. Student affairs professionals can assist parents in understanding why we may desire to use a student-learning model in a given situation when the parents expect a customer-service model to be operating.

The Importance of an Institutional Philosophy for the Role of Parents

The issues surrounding the role of parents as partners in the educational process have become sufficiently complex as to require greater visibility within our institutional cultures. Parents are an increasingly important constituency in recruitment, retention, fundraising, and public relations, as well as student affairs. Our institutions are best served if internal constituencies can speak with a clear and consistent

voice about the appropriate role of parents in the institutional context. A clear and consistent articulation of the institutional philosophy should achieve several goals. It should set expectations for students and parents. It should invite parents to participate and establish appropriate boundaries around their involvement. Finally, it should acknowledge the pressures that parents feel and give them some clear guidance about how best to respond when their students have difficulties. In addition, it may acknowledge a continuum of levels of engagement that parents have with different functions within our administrative structures. For example, at opposite ends of the spectrum, the financial aid office may choose to direct most of its communications directly to parents, whereas the health and counseling offices are under legal constraints regarding sharing information without student consent. Legal constraints, administrative convenience and efficiency, student development, and student learning are all part of the institutional philosophy regarding parents. These components are likely to be present in each of our institutional philosophies. The emphasis may vary, depending on institutional history and type, student demographics, and even region of the country. Determining how all these variables come together in a particular institutional context is the essence of an institutional philosophy.

Student Affairs Administrators as Catalysts

Bringing visibility and focus to current issues is a growing aspect of our roles as student affairs administrators. We are well-positioned within the institution to bring clarity and focus to the issue of understanding today's parents. We can be especially helpful in this role because of our value-based perspective that keeps the student at the center of the equation. Our training and experience in student affairs provide us with the skill and capacity to integrate different perspectives and negotiate conflicts. We have firsthand knowledge of the roles that parents can play, positively and negatively, in their students' experiences. Student affairs administrators also tend to have a good understanding of campus networks; student affairs staff excels in its ability to see the campus as a connected network of intersecting relationships. Work with parents is cross-divisional work; in many institutions, no one office or division is "in charge" of parent relationships. Traditionally, student affairs practitioners are recognized for their ability to forge relationships and do collaborative work. "We can bring individuals who do not know each other into relationship, or we can facilitate new alliances or cooperative ventures with others" (Allen & Cherry, 2000, p. 31). These skills and aptitudes make student affairs professionals natural leaders in crafting a consistent institutional philosophy in working with parents.

Navigating the Campus Political Environment

Virtually every administrative, business, athletic, and academic function within the college interfaces with parents regularly, and each unit brings its own perspective to its work with this important constituency. As consumers of higher education, parents are likely to contact the institution at any level they believe could be helpful or influential to their situation. In many instances, parents will circumvent the college entirely and contact the governor; a national, state, or local legislator; a member of the institutional governing board; or even the media to present their concern. Student affairs professionals are often confronted with requests for exceptions or special treatment, and the sources of the requests vary greatly. A faculty member may call the director of orientation to ask that her daughter be able to register for classes without attending the required orientation program. A congressional representative may intervene for a family in an admissions decision. The president's chief of staff may request a special residence hall assignment for the son of a trustee well after the deadline has passed and all rooms have been assigned. A significant donor may ask that the college not continue to pursue hazing allegations against the son of a friend. An alumna may demand a change in a sorority recruitment decision that affects her daughter. A minister may request that a student not be required to live on campus because of the perceived permissive atmosphere in the college residence halls.

Student affairs staff members are not the only ones who receive numerous requests from parents or their

influential friends for special treatment for students. The president's office, of course, receives many calls from parents and others who prefer to "start at the top and work their way down" to resolve an issue. The chief development officer is another prime target as parents use their potential financial influence on fundraising efforts as leverage to receive special consideration. Surprisingly, faculty and academic administrators are now having to respond to parents who are upset about grades or treatment of their students in the classroom. Trustees are often asked to use their influence on behalf of parents to insure that a request is granted. It seems that no one on or off the campus is immune from a potential parental request.

Institutional constituencies may react differently to parental concerns or requests due to philosophical, legal, administrative, financial, or political reasons. In student affairs, staff members who subscribe to either a student-development or student-learning perspective in working with students may want parents, or their representatives, to understand the value of the student being his/her own advocate. Parental intervention often thwarts the opportunity for the student to learn from a potentially negative experience or to develop the skills necessary to resolve issues in the future.

Not long ago, two residence hall roommates were not getting along so one of them was given permission to move up one floor to a different room. When he moved, he took his former roommate's DVD player with him to his new room. Student affairs staff hoped the former roommates would resolve the problem between themselves or with the help of the resident assistant; unfortunately, that was not the case. One young man e-mailed his mother who e-mailed the mother of the student who moved who e-mailed her son to ask that he return the DVD player. Many student affairs professionals frequently express concern for the lack of proficiency of students' conflict-resolution skills; parental intervention may impede the student learning that can occur through resolution of conflict experiences.

Student development and student learning also suffer when parents choose to become involved in the decisions that college administrators make. For example, a student is not selected to be an orientation leader, and in her notification letter she is told that she may see the director for feedback on her interview. Instead of seeing the director, she tells her parents, and her father calls demanding to know why his daughter was not selected. What could have been an important and informative conversation between student and orientation director is now a guarded defense of the director's decision, and unfortunately, no student learning occurs. Student passivity may be reinforced by parental intervention. Student affairs professionals find themselves caught in conflict between a polite and professional customer-service response to parents and a gnawing sense of actually undermining more critical, albeit more abstract, learning goals for the individual student.

Legal issues often create barriers that parents do not understand or accept. (Extensive discussion of these issues is provided in Chapter 6. The protections provided student records under the Family Educational Rights and Privacy Act (FERPA) and how an institution interprets the law create perhaps the greatest concerns for parents. Some institutions do not provide academic information to parents of dependent students even though FERPA allows for this communication to occur. From preschool through high school, parents have had access to their student's academic records, but in college are often told that the grades belong to the student. Parents are counseled to speak with their student, but often react with, "I am paying the bills; I have a right to see the grades!" Not only do parents want to see the grades, some believe it is their duty to contact a faculty member to have a grade changed. New faculty often chuckle during their orientation program when they are told that parents will be calling them, only to find out that the calls do occur. How faculty members choose to handle these calls can have a rippling impact on other departments or divisions. A few years ago, an angry mother called student affairs to complain about a faculty member (actually a department chair) whom, she believed, was rude and inappropriate when she called about her daughter's grade in the class. The daughter had received an *F* and the mother did not believe, for many reasons, that she deserved an *F*. The faculty member agreed

with her, explaining however, that an *F* was the lowest grade he was allowed to record and thus he'd had to give her daughter an *F* for the course!

Medical, psychological and judicial issues also present legal and/or ethical concerns for staff when parents call. A health center physician or a psychologist in the counseling center must function within professional ethics regarding how and with whom they may share information. Explaining these guidelines to parents during orientation doesn't mean that they won't call. Again, parents are accustomed to having access to this information about their student, and they expect to continue to be fully informed. Allegations of violations of the college's judicial code may also spark some parent interest, and judicial officers are often placed on the defensive in these interactions. Attorneys may be called, and they expect to represent the student in the proceedings, only to learn that their role is limited to that of advisor. Attempts by parents, attorneys, and even presidents to influence judicial outcomes on behalf of students are not uncommon.

Occasionally, parents will overtly ask a student affairs staff member to violate the law on behalf of their student. One former chief student affairs officer spoke of the seemingly annual call he would get once roommate pairings were provided to students. The call would come from a parent and would usually begin with, "I believe you have made a terrible mistake." The parent had just learned that his or her student had been assigned a roommate of a different ethnic background and would demand a change quickly and quietly.

Development officers are particularly vulnerable to parental requests for influence of campus decisions, because money and relationships speak loudly to institutions of higher education. One well-known institution recently acknowledged that it favored the children of large donors in the admissions process, a practice more common than the public would like to believe. It is not unusual for a chief student affairs officer to receive a call from a counterpart in development or from the office of the president requesting a favor for a parent who also happens to be a donor. Many institutions favor legacies (sons and daughters of alumni) in admissions decisions, which tend to create an expectation of admission in the minds of all alumni. These parents may use whatever leverage they can to insure that the family tradition of enrollment in a particular college continues. It may be only natural for legacy parents to then expect favoritism to continue in the spheres of housing, class assignments, and resolution of student problems.

Closely allied with the ethical dilemmas faced by development staff are public relations officers who are extremely sensitive to the perceptions of the influential public, especially the media. Parents are quick to react when the press learns of an allegation of serious misconduct by a college student, especially if their own student is mentioned. Public relations professionals want problems to go away quickly with minimal damage to the institutional image, while student affairs staff would advocate following established processes developed to support student learning.

Student affairs staff professionals occasionally find themselves in a philosophical conflict with their colleagues in business affairs regarding parental interaction and involvement. Some institutions send tuition, housing, meal plan, and other bills to parents, while other colleges send via electronic mail all official correspondence, including grades, directly to students. At a number of colleges, the business affairs staff sends letters to parents explaining that all billing will go to their students' local addresses or e-mail accounts, but that they may ask their students to share their PINs and passwords so that parents can access the students' billing information (as well as academic grades). Student affairs staff, on the other hand, typically encourages students to communicate important financial information to their parents so that deadlines are not missed, placing the responsibility with the students, not the parents. With either approach, the goal is to have parents and students discussing these matters with each other, instead of parents attempting to gain this information from the institution.

Given the myriad of issues and players involved in working with parents and other constituencies, how can student affairs staff appropriately influence campus decisions and decision makers in the best interest of the students as well as the institution?

Crafting an Institutional Philosophy Regarding Working with Parents

As important as it is for an institution to develop a comprehensive philosophy about its relationship with parents, it is a rare college that has done so through an intentional, cognitive process. More likely, an institutional culture of how to respond to and communicate with parents develops over time and varies between divisions and academic units across campus. Thus, as parents interact with admissions staff, faculty, judicial officers, residence life staff, or administrators, they often receive confusing, even conflicting information. "Higher education institutions can, and often do, unintentionally perpetuate a parental identity crisis. Murky guidelines for family involvement lead to inconsistent interactions from campus to campus, and more alarmingly, from office to office on the same campus" (Daniel, Evans, & Scott, 2001, p. 4). Besides the obvious drawbacks for the institution, this type of campus culture encourages parents to move from one office to another in an attempt to get different, perceived to be better, responses to their requests.

At a recent national workshop on this topic, one of us asked how many of the participants' colleges have a philosophy about working with parents. Only one hand went up from the audience, but as discussion continued, it became clear that every institution represented in the room had a philosophy guiding their efforts with parents, a philosophy that was implicit and "just understood" rather than explicit and intentionally communicated to staff. Clearly, someone on a campus needs to begin the discussion which can result in a cohesive, agreed-upon guiding philosophy for working with today's college parents. Student affairs staff members are good candidates for this task. They can begin by conducting focus groups with a range of campus constituencies to gauge how the institution is interfacing with parents, conducting an internal audit of current practices for communication with parents to see how parents are encouraged (or discouraged) to engage with the college and its programs, and identifying staff members' concerns and frustrations with these issues. It is important to include at least one representative from the president's office in these discussions as that office typically sets the tone and expectations for staff interactions with parents. "With over four thousand institutions of higher education across the country, it is improbable if not impossible to define a single college-student family relationship" (Daniel et al., 2001, p. 10). This fact does not diminish the importance of each institution clarifying its relationship with parents and communicating that information in an intentional way to all faculty, staff, and administrators.

A committee composed of student affairs staff, faculty, development and alumni officers, business and finance administrators, parents, and others can conduct the work necessary to develop an institutional philosophy to guide the college's work with parents. An important part of this effort is for all members of the group to share perspectives and goals for working with parents. Ultimately, our institutions must gain a better understanding of how differing priorities are resolved on our campuses. The task is not an easy one and calls for a serious investment in listening, collaboration, and compromise. A draft of the philosophy should be shared internally with all interested constituencies so that those with a vested interest in the philosophy can provide feedback to the committee. Expect the language of the written philosophy to undergo many revisions before reaching a final version acceptable to the entire campus.

Once a philosophy has been developed, identified, and agreed upon, it can provide the foundation for staff development and training, as well as be the guiding principle for content development of parent programs, publications, and events. A simple, straightforward philosophy might be to work together to create a successful college experience for every student. Another approach might be to facilitate parents and students in the transition of their relationship from parent-child to parent-college student, and eventually to parent-independent college graduate. Staff benefits from training based on the institution's philosophy through group discussion, case studies, and opportunities to share experiences and concerns with colleagues. The philosophy should appear in parent publications and be a part of orientation for new parent/family

association officers or parent council members. It should explicitly and implicitly be communicated both internally to campus constituencies and externally to parents and families. Having this identified, agreed-upon philosophy for college-parent relationships increases the ease and accuracy of communication and lessens confusion and anxiety for all involved.

The Impact of Institutional Type On Parent Relationships

Institutional type, size, mission, and geographic location may shape how staff and faculty at a college approach their work with parents. In a previous section in this chapter, we mentioned actual scenarios involving parents which we had experienced or observed. Because higher education institutions are so diverse in their nature, the reaction to or resolution of these scenarios would likely differ from college to college. The one constant, however, is that the general tone and direction for working with parents will be set at the presidential level. For example, if the president wants parents to receive a *yes* as the college's answer to whatever their request might be, then size, type, mission, and location may not matter as much to the staff and faculty who respond to parents.

Parents do not view a college through an organizational chart, so they are most likely to contact someone with whom they have established a relationship (or the president). Chief student affairs officers work diligently to keep problems/concerns/issues from reaching the desk of the president, so it is recommended that they designate a staff member to be visible and available to parents as a point of initial contact with the institution. The orientation director in any size or type of institution can be helpful by showcasing the person (or persons) who will be the primary parent contact once students are enrolled.

It is our experience that large public institutions, especially flagship universities, tend to receive the greatest public scrutiny. Many decisions and issues at these universities are debated publicly and widely by legislators, alumni, trustees, parents, the media, faculty, and others. There appears to be a genuine feeling of ownership and pride by each constituency. This can be a mixed blessing, as institutional successes are widely celebrated, while negative situations may be severely criticized. These institutions must operate in an open environment recognizing that virtually every document may be subject to an open records request. Parents of students at these schools see themselves as both taxpaying citizens and consumers, and they expect the institution to be responsive to their concerns. In addition, parents of students in large institutions want assurance that their student is not an anonymous number.

Private colleges, on the other hand, are usually not subject to the same level of public scrutiny or as accountable to the general public and the media as their public counterparts. Parents of students in these institutions, however, have high expectations as consumers, as they are paying a larger share of the cost of their student's education. These institutions tend to work diligently to keep parents satisfied with the educational experience students receive. The spoken or unspoken philosophy of handling parent issues may differ in the private college setting due to the perceived and real economic importance of the parent constituency.

By comparison, small colleges typically take great pride in the personal attention they provide to students, and this attention may extend to parents as well. These colleges, both public and private, tend to endorse the concepts of family and partnership in their relationships with students and parents. For staff and faculty, the small size of the college enhances their ability to know and communicate with one another, so if there is an operating institutional philosophy for working with parents, it is likely well known throughout the college. Parental expectations for special attention and consideration of issues important to their student's success are generally understood and respected at small colleges.

We believe that institutional location can also be a factor in the relationship between parents and the college. Is the college located in a rural area with a very traditional-age student body that is primarily from out of state? Is it a large, diverse urban institution?

Is it a community college located in a suburban area that attracts primarily adult students? Is it a large flagship institution located in a "college town?" The issues for parents and the relationship the college develops with parents may differ in each of these locations. It is important, therefore, that institutions are intentional in their approaches to parent programs and parent relationships. What messages are delivered to parents in orientation—"Welcome to our family;" or "We want to develop a partnership with you;" or "We want to work with your student to help him/her develop the knowledge and skills he/she will need to be successful"? How will the institution continue its communication with parents once students are enrolled—"We will be corresponding with you if your student is caught drinking;" or "As a member of our Parents and Families Association, you will receive regular newsletters, and we hope you will attend our fall weekend for parents;" or "Our philosophy is to communicate with your student, and we expect your student to communicate with you"? The one constant message that institutions should convey is that the college invites parents to partner with the staff and faculty in an effort to provide students with maximum opportunities for academic and personal success.

> Colleges may have no choice about whether they will deal with parents, but when it comes to *how* they interact with this important and influential group, they have many options. Each institution should develop goals and programs that engage parents appropriately and beneficially in the education of their sons and daughters. (Johnson, 2004, p. B11)

Suggestions for Resolving Concerns or Problems Raised by Parents

The foundation for responding to parent concerns is laid at parent orientation when the appropriate speaker discusses the transitions both parents and students experience during the first year of college, as well as the institution's philosophy for its relationship with parents. This is our first opportunity to define and explain our relationship with our students' parents. Parents' changing role in their students' lives could be described as a shift from caretaker and supervisor to that of encourager, mentor, and coach. Parents should be assured that they will continue to have tremendous influence on their college students, but it also could be pointed out that they will no longer have day-to-day veto power over every choice their students make. Parents can be encouraged to channel their support and interest in their students' college experience in appropriate and helpful ways, and all this information can be reinforced through parent newsletters, electronic mail messages, parent listservs, etc. Laying this foundation at the earliest opportunity and then revisiting it through ongoing communication makes the task of responding to parent concerns considerably easier.

We need to educate the people we work with on our campuses as well. Student affairs leadership should anticipate situations that might cause parents to make requests or lodge complaints with the institution's president, development officers, governing trustees, legislators, or state governor. In an ideal world, we would not be asked for special favors by any of these individuals, but for most of us, these requests are part of the job. What we can do is set parameters on these requests. For example, if we know that each summer the president's office will be asked to secure specific housing assignments for sons/daughters/friends of influential people, we can anticipate these requests and set aside a certain number of rooms for political assignments. We can then inform the president's office that this has been done, and let them know when they've used up all but one or two of their special assignments. By collaborating with the offices that typically make special requests for parents, it is possible to shape and limit these types of requests. In other contexts, it may be appropriate to visit with the president or vice president for development privately to gently remind them of the negative repercussions that such acts of favoritism create on campus.

We also can prepare our staff for its work with parents. It is only recently that some graduate preparation programs even mention parents as a constituency that new professionals will encounter in their work. Too often, staff knows little of the characteristics of today's college parents, their expectations of higher education, or how best to respond to their needs and concerns. When staff members have an understanding of

parents, they can anticipate issues and concerns and can prepare accordingly. By adding basic, quality, customer-service training components, staff will feel empowered to respond appropriately to parent requests, concerns, and complaints.

Training components to prepare staff for its work with parents might include some of the following:

1. Reviewing the institution's relationship with parents and families: how the college defines its role with parents, how best to convey student development theory and its impact on the college's relationship with parents.

2. Using case studies to provide staff opportunities to practice communicating specific policies and processes to parents from an educational or student development framework.

3. Discussing situations—housing and roommate assignments, Greek recruitment, etc.—that typically generate parent questions and concerns, and consideration of appropriate responses to both internal and external constituencies.

4. Exchanging observations and concerns about today's college parents.

5. Showcasing staff with experience and skill in working with parents.

6. Offering specific guidelines for responding to parent calls.

7. Providing training for managing angry or emotionally distraught parent calls. Training should be ongoing and should include front-line support staff. Examples of training materials can be found at the end of this chapter.

Concluding Thoughts

In this chapter, the authors have attempted to explore the issue of partnership with parents of today's college students by discussing why and how parents intervene in the lives of their students, the importance of an institutional philosophy for working with parents, how student affairs professionals can assume leadership in crafting an institutional philosophy, and ways that parental concerns can be resolved. Training materials for staff have also been presented.

There are a number of reasons why it makes educational sense for the college to provide clearly defined opportunities for parents to stay involved in their student's academic experience. The underlying aim in student development theory and practice is to provide an educational environment that acknowledges the multidimensional aspects of human development and strives to enhance the growth process. (Austin, 2003, p.137).

By taking the lead to provide structure and boundaries to the parent/college relationship through the development of an institutional philosophy for working with parents, student affairs administrators can proactively position their institutions to partner with this challenging and enjoyable constituency while maximizing the potential for academic and personal success of students.

References

Allen, K. & Cherry, C. (2000). *Systemic leadership.* Lanham, MD: University Press of America.

Austin, D. M. (2003). The role of family influence on student success. In J. A. Ward-Roof and C. Hatch (Eds.), *Designing successful transitions: A guide for orienting students to college* (2nd ed.). Columbia, SC: National Resource Center for the First-Year Experience and Students in Transition.

Daniel, B. V., Evans, S. G., & Scott, B. R. (2001). Understanding family involvement in the college experience today. In B. V. Daniel and B. R. Scott (Eds.), *Consumers, adversaries and partners: Working with the families of undergraduates.* San Francisco: Jossey Bass.

Johnson, H. E. (2004). Educating parents about college life. *The Chronicle of Higher Education, 50*(18), B11.

Chapter 2
Changing Demographics and Diversity in Higher Education

Renee Barnett Terry, Charlene M. Dukes, Laura E. Valdez, and Andrew Wilson

Over the next decade, campuses will become more diverse. Moreover, a different generation of students and families pose new issues. Understanding the cultural background and diversity of these students and their families remains vital to the partnering with students and families. This chapter will focus on the characteristics of some of these groups that reflect the diverse student populations entering higher education and the familial influences on their lives. Specifically, the chapter examines students and families of this generation along with students who identify as African American; Latino; Native American; Asian Pacific; international; gay, lesbian, bisexual, and transgender (GLBT); and students with disabilities and their families.

Obviously, each group possesses individual differences. Hopefully, broadly describing experiences documented in the literature will assist practitioners in their overall practice with the rapidly changing student demographics. We do caution readers that individual differences impact experiences and, therefore, the needs of this evolving population.

Millennial Students and Their Families

Millennial students first arrived on college campuses in the fall of 2000, according to Strauss and Howe (2000). This new wave of students, also labeled the Internet generation (Tapscott, 1997), Nexters, and Generation Y, was born on or after 1982. They differ from their most immediate predecessors, the Gen Xers (born 1961-1981). The millennials' parents belong primarily to the baby-boomer generation (born 1943-1960).

Strauss and Howe (2003) describe the millennial student as special, sheltered, confident, team-oriented, conventional, pressured and achieving. Growing up in the '80s and '90s, the millennials are the largest and most affluent group when compared to any previous

generation. Millennials have high levels of comfort with the Internet, diverse populations, and tragedies (e.g., Columbine, September 11). As students, millennials have been actively involved in school-sponsored cocurricular and academic programs throughout their lives.

As millennial students go to college, they come with more exposure to their parents and adults overall. They tend to have frequent communication and positive relationships with their parents (Trice, 2002). Millennials often seek parents for advice rather than independently making decisions. Millennials and their parents have benefited from technological advances that allow for greater connectivity and communication (e.g., cell phones, instant messages, and e-mails).

Although millennials have increased contact with their parents, many of them face certain challenges. For example, millennials experience exceptionally high stress and anxiety compared to previous generations of college students (Murray, 1997). Millennial students present challenges to college staff and faculty as many are arriving with serious psychological issues, misusing prescription drugs, and feeling pressured to excel.

Parents of millennial students have certain hopes that their children will excel and have high expectations of higher education. These parents are members of the baby-boomer generation that has left an indelible mark. Baby boomers aided in reshaping American institutions such as education, music, television, political activism, social awareness, and economic largesse. Technology and medical research have blossomed throughout the lives of this generation. Specifically, public education was reinvented to meet their needs (i.e., greater access and increased number of degrees produced).

Sometimes referred to as *helicopter parents,* parents of millennial students tend to hover over every aspect of their student's lives. These parents have engaged their students in different ways; for instance, parents and teachers have worked closely together from preschool through high school to support student success. The paradigm shift for parents and students that higher education does not allow for the same involvement level remains a challenge. Moreover, parents of millennials have high expectations for their students, including attending and graduating from college. They believe that a college education leads to better jobs and increased income (Wilgoren, 2000).

Millennials also represent the greatest increase in diversity of any previous generation. Increasing numbers of African-American, Asian, Native-American, and Hispanic/Latino students; first-generation students; students with at least one immigrant parent; and students identifying as GLBT are enrolling at colleges and universities. As a result, generalizations about the parents of these students are difficult, but some overarching themes emerge that impact the work of higher education professionals. Millennials' parents have higher expectations of colleges and universities than their predecessors, expect greater involvement in decisions that impact their students, and demand rapid and favorable institutional responses to their concerns. Overall, these parents raise the bar on parental involvement in higher education.

African-American Students and Their Families

During the past 50 years, African Americans have gained significant access to higher education institutions due to such landmark events as the *Brown v. Board of Education* decision in 1954 and the Higher Education Act of 1965. Consequently, among African Americans, more believe a college education is a necessity to increase their standard of living. The majority of African-American parents are convinced that a college education is more important now than in the past. They also believe that the high price of a college education should not keep qualified students from pursuing higher education (Garibaldi, 1997). The number of African-American students enrolled in college has risen steadily over the past 20 years. Specifically, the number of African Americans enrolled in college in 1980 was 1,106,800 compared to 1,640,700 in 1999 (Horn, Peter, Rooney, & Malizio, (2002).

Higher education is perceived as the admission ticket to good jobs and a middle-class lifestyle. African-American parents frequently spoke of higher education as the key to economic and social mobility, and as one possible way to overcome the barriers of poverty and prejudice (Immerwahr & Foleno, 2000).

While higher education continues to serve as a staple for combating societal barriers for success, Hairston (2000) provides several emerging influences on the success of African-American students in college: (a) desire to imitate parents' altruistic behavior and role as community contributors, (b) high academic and career expectations by parents, (c) parental support in academic and occupational endeavors, (d) parents providing early exposure to vocational subject matter and/or the teaching field, and (e) parents aiding in the discovery of aptitudes and interests in vocational subject matter.

The study emphasizes that the value parents place on higher education becomes even more striking when compared to actual participation rates of the various groups. Participation in higher education is lowest among Hispanics, somewhat higher among African Americans and highest among Whites. Significantly, the value placed on college education is highest among those who have the lowest rates of participation. Hispanics, who have the lowest participation rates, are the most likely to stress the importance of higher education (Immerwahr & Foleno, 2000).

Latino Students and Their Families

Latinos vary greatly in ethnicity, country of origin, immigration patterns, socioeconomic status, and level of education. Historically, Latinos are family-oriented or collectivistic with a commitment to the group compared to non-Latinos who tend to be individualistic (Padilla, Treviño, Gonzalez, & Treviño, 1997). This familial commitment may result in Latino students who defer to parental authority rather than make individual choices, value birth order, and prioritize familial interests versus individual needs. Typically, family plays a central part in Latino students' college experience.

When students move away from home, Latino students will seek a "family" on campus for a supportive college experience (Padilla et al., 1997). Building trust and nurturing relationships with students moving far from home to attend college is particularly important. Families need to see that students connect through mentors, roommates, multicultural center staff, or other student affairs professionals. Parents may have additional angst regarding the college process because the student will be outside the family nest. Latinos have also historically respected adult authority because they embrace the philosophy that everyone in the child's community takes part in shaping the child's values, morals, and behaviors. For example, grandparents, aunts, uncles, godparents, priests, nuns, and neighbors all have responsibilities in raising a child along with the parents.

Given some of these broad generic traits, student affairs professionals' role with the Latino student and their families may be uniquely significant possess a unique significance. Some Latino families entrust that college officials will intervene in the student's life as a family member. Many Latino parents will leave a college representative "in charge" of their student. Unlike some other groups, Latino parents may embrace the in loco parentis philosophy.

While some Latino students may move away from their family home to attend college, other Latino students continue living at home. As a result, these off-campus Latino students might not seek out relationships to substitute for family support, but will seek relationships to simply cope with college. Often these students will continue to shoulder many family responsibilities while attending college. Parents of Latinos that have strong desires to remain close to family may influence their children to attend the local, public university or community college, which will allow the student to live at home and continue to contribute to the family.

Some families might not realize the demands of college and may maintain family responsibilities. Latina students in particular have higher gender role conflicts based on parental expectations (Rodriguez, Guido-DiBrito, Torres, & Talbot, 2000). During student orientation programs, college officials may assist family members in understanding the need to shift duties, particularly during stressful parts of the term.

Engaging family members with the institution may ease the transition for Latino students and families. Family involvement stems from the valuing of family, so parents remain the source of encouragement and support, as opposed to the hovering parent that supports the student by doing things for them. Student affairs professionals should engage the Latino family to promote comfort in and increase understanding of the complexities of pursuing a college education.

Native-American Students and Their Families

Native-American students represent many tribal nations that do not have a common language, religion, or geographic location. Some shared values have been identified in the literature, such as spirituality, child rearing, family, and group harmony (HeavyRunner & Morris, 1997). Native Americans in higher education represent a small number at most institutions, so they are often invisible in reports or research studies. Native-American students represent only 153,845 (U.S. Department of Education, 2004, Table 1) of the overall college population and only 0.9% (U.S. Department of Education, 2004, Table 9) of undergraduates in research institutions.

Research about Native-American students' resilience revealed that the family is a major source of motivation to succeed in college (Reyhner & Dodd, 1995, p. 5; Dodd, Garcia, Meccage, & Nelson, 1995, p. 75). Traditional Native-American families include extended blood relatives and clan relations, and they share the responsibility of child rearing (HeavyRunner & Morris, 1997).

Native-American students tend to be older, married (Dodd et al., 1995), or single parents. Thus, numerous family obligations may interfere with their education (Tate & Schwartz, 1993). These students take longer to receive their degrees, but nonetheless some students are motivated to graduate to help improve the lives of their children and to give back to their communities.

Amongst Navajo college graduates, family remained the most significant single factor in influencing students' academic achievement (Rindone, 1988). Most of the Navajo families studied earned low incomes and they predominately spoke the Navajo language at home. Navajo parents usually possessed only grade-school educations and practiced traditional religious traditions. Similarly, students studied from the Sioux tribe were dependent upon the retention of cultural identity and heritage that fostered a strong sense of confidence and personal self-identity (Huffman, Sill, & Brokenleg, 1986).

The limited literature on Native-American students suggests that because these students are firmly grounded in their culture and connected to traditional parents, they can continuously persist in higher education, despite the fact that high levels of socioeconomic status and education are predictors of success for other students. Moreover, Native-American students travel home more often than nonnative students to take part in ceremonies or help family on weekends, which may prevent participation in extracurricular activities and adversely affect class attendance (Cibik & Chambers, 1991). Such experiences may help students remain connected to their extended family, which strengthens their cultural identity.

In efforts to work closely with Native-American students and their families, student affairs practitioners might utilize a model developed by the tribal colleges in Montana. Recognizing that a family-centered approach helps students' perseverance, the Family Education Model includes culturally specific, family, on-campus activities, counseling strategies that include family issues, and seminars or workshops on family-life skills (HeavyRunner & Marshall, 2003). This model effectively engages family members as partners in the students' educational process.

Asian Pacific-American Students and Their Families

Asian Pacific-American students represent one of the most diverse student populations in higher education and the fastest-growing racial group in higher education today. Specifically, this population represents over 57 different ethnic groups (McEwen, Kodama, Alvarez, Lee, & Liang, 2002), including representation at U.S. colleges and universities by Chinese (25%), Korean (13%), Vietnamese (13%), Japanese (11%), Asian Indians (11%), Filipinos (11%), and others (16%) including Native Hawaiians, Laotians, Hmong, Thais, Samoans, Sri Lankans, Indonesians, Pakistanis, and Bangladeshis (Horn et al., 2002). According to the 2000 census data, 68.9% of Asian Americans were foreign-born (Special Tabulations, Figure 5), most speak a language other than English (Summary File 3), and almost half or 49% (Summary File 1) live in the western part of the U.S. (U.S. Census Bureau, 2003). According to the U.S. National Center for Education Statistics (2002, Table 207), Asian Pacific-American students represented over 6% of enrollment in colleges and universities in the U.S. in 2000 with a higher percentage of women enrolled compared to men.

Asian Pacific-American students are often characterized as the "model minority" (Suzuki, 2002, p. 21) because they are viewed as highly driven to achieve academically, financially, and largely influenced through strong parental values. The perpetuation of this stereotype as the high achiever who has no problems or issues may result in the neglect of their needs as students on campus and increased feelings of invalidation as a student (Suzuki, 2002).

Asian Pacific-American students are significantly influenced by their parents and families, as academic success and achievement are important values of the community (Kim, Atkinson, & Yang, 1999). For example, these parents strongly affect their students' decisions to attend college (Choe, 1998) and selection of career choices (Leong & Serafica, 1995). Of all ethnic groups, Asian Pacific-American students consider parental pressure as one of the top influences in making their career decisions (Leong, 1995). Largely influenced by their parents, Asian Pacific-American students select more science and technology occupations than other college student populations (Leong & Serafica, 1995). Choosing majors in the sciences, health care, business, and engineering areas might be linked to issues related to academic achievement related to prestige and financial security for their families (Louie, 2001). Furthermore, parental expectations affect these students' abilities to change majors in college despite changes in the personal or academic interests of students (McEwen et al., 2002). Some Asian Pacific-American students experience extreme stress and alienation due to exceptionally high expectations by their parents (Wong & Mock, 1997).

Family responsibility and support are fundamental cultural values, but not meeting such high expectations may result in loss of support from students' families and communities (Yeh & Huang, 1996). Achievement is viewed as a family accomplishment and Asian Pacific-American students comply with their parents' wishes to bring fame to their families (Hsia & Peng, 1998). Family, culture, and parental involvement in the achievement of Asian Pacific-American college students are significant aspects of these students' higher education experience.

International Students and Their Families

Recent visa regulations have slowed the enrollment growth of foreign students in U.S. colleges and universities. International students enroll in community colleges, undergraduate programs in 4-year institutions, as well as graduate programs. Community colleges have enjoyed a 61.3% enrollment growth in international students since 1993 (Institute of International Education, 2002, p. 13).

International students often face diverse challenges such as adjusting to a different educational system, cultural differences, and language challenges (Zhai, 2002). International students and their families may not access campus resources as frequently as other students. For example, international students more often turn to family and friends for help rather than use on-campus counseling due to the difficulty associated with sharing personal concerns with a virtual stranger (Zhai, 2002).

Since families are likely to be far from the host institution, they are also less likely to work closely with administrators. These family members face considerable challenges as well, similar to those of their students. Understanding the American educational system may be difficult, accepting how their student acclimates to a new culture may be disturbing, and language barriers with the new country may increase communication concerns. Since most of these family members do not attend a college orientation program, providing support services for these students, especially at the beginning of their college experience, is critical. Support services staff might attempt to be persistent in reaching out to international students, so they can be encouraged to utilize college resources.

Gay, Lesbian, Bisexual, and Transgender Students and Their Families

More students than ever are arriving on college campuses identifying as GLBT (S. Chestnut, personal communication, November 14, 2003). Diverse and heterogeneous, many GLBT students feel unwelcome and isolated on college and university campuses. Rhoads (1997) found that most of the challenges faced by members of this community are related to coming-out, visibility, harassment, and discrimination concerns. Coming-out to parents and friends as members of this community can be psychologically difficult (Fontaine & Hammond, 1996) and generally is accompanied by major life disruptions and challenges (Fontaine & Hammond, 1996).

GLBT students struggle fitting into collegiate life throughout their student tenure (Wall & Evans, 2000). Widespread homophobia existed in university communities with 98% of freshmen having heard disparaging comments toward lesbians or gay men (D'Augelli & Rose, 1990, p. 488). Not only do GLBT students hear hostile language, but also experience fear for their personal safety on many campuses (Kaplan & Colbs, 2000). With increasing numbers of students arriving at college already identifying as gay, researchers must look closer at how to mitigate these environmental circumstances and help practitioners better prepare for this new trend.

According to studies of gay, lesbian, and bisexual (GLB) youth, more than half reported that their parents rejected their sexual orientation (Hetrick & Martin, 1987, p. 23). Additionally, students from other underrepresented groups such as African American, Latino, and Asian American must balance racial identity development along with their sexual identity development.

Support for GLBT students on campus is offered through centers, student organizations, campus allies, and organizations such as Parents and Friends of Lesbians and Gays (PFLAG). Role models are sought and needed in the campus community by GLBT students, as most parents do not share the same sexual identity and do not serve as role models compared to their heterosexual counterparts (Kraig, 1998). A supportive campus environment with administrators, faculty, and students working to create an inclusive environment which is safe, respectful, and welcoming of all its members is critically needed on every campus, and particularly for the GLBT community which continues to fight for such an environment in the university community.

Disabled Students and Their Families

As discussed throughout this monograph, the transition to an adult-to-adult relationship for college students and their families can be a challenging and rewarding process on a number of different levels. For the 9% of postsecondary students with a disability (National Center for Educational Statistics, 2003, Table 211) and their family members, this transition brings with it a unique background of often intense involvement in the student's education.

The evolution of special education programs and the advent of the Americans with Disabilities Act of 1990 have allowed the family members of students with disabilities the opportunity to be intimately involved in their student's education and development. Based on the extent and severity of a student's disability, families will have met with a host of medical professionals and

specialists regarding diagnosis and treatment, and a gauntlet of school administrators and teachers in the development of their student's individual education plan. As students make their transition into the environment of higher education, the exhilaration of independence and management of their own affairs may precipitate additional anxiety for their family members.

Hameister (1989) challenged institutions to follow the tenets of developmental theory in supporting students with disabilities. Encouraging independence, supporting the mainstreaming of freshmen with disabilities, seeking input from students in developing services, and recognizing the individual nature of each student's circumstance provide a reasonable framework for supporting students. Providing family members with an overview of services provided and an education in the development theory applied in the delivery of these services can be an essential step in supporting student success and independence.

Concluding Comments

This chapter is intended to give the reader a sense of some of the issues facing student affairs professionals as they embrace the needs of the families of an extremely diverse student population. Not only do today's students represent increasing diversity in higher education, but also their family structures and traditions provide staff with new challenges and opportunities that impact services and programs. There are many more examples of diversity among students and parents/family members than those discussed in this chapter, but hopefully we have captured the essence of the changing scene and its impact on the work of student affairs staff.

Authors' note: David Brunnemer, director disability resources for students, Western Washington University, assisted with the section on disabled students and their families.

References

Choe, Y. L. (1998). *Exploring the experiences of Asian students at the University of Virginia.* Unpublished manuscript.

Cibik, M. A. & Chambers, S. L. (1991). Similarities and differences among Native Americans, Hispanics, Blacks, and Anglos. *National Association of Student Personnel Administrators Journal, 28*(2), 129-39.

D'Augelli, A. R. & Rose, M. L. (1990). Homophobia in a university community: Attitudes and experiences of heterosexual freshmen. *Journal of College Student Development, 31,* 484-491.

Dodd, J. M., Garcia, F. M., Meccage, C., & Nelson, J. R. (1995). American Indian Student Retention. *National Association of Student Personnel Administrators Journal, 33*(1), 72-78.

Fontaine, J. H, & Hammond, N. L. (1996). Counseling issues with gay and lesbian adolescents. *Adolescence, 31,* 817-30.

Garibaldi, A. M. (1997). Four decades of progress . . . and decline: An assessment of African-American educational attainment. *Journal of Negro Education, 66*(2), 105-120.

Hairston, J. (2000). How parents influence African-American students' decision to prepare for vocational teaching careers. *Journal of Career and Technical Education, 16*(2).

Hameister, B. G. (1989). Disabled students. In M. L. Upcraft, J. N. Gardner, & Associates, *The freshman year experience: Helping students survive and succeed in college* (pp. 340-351). San Francisco: Jossey-Bass.

HeavyRunner, I. & Sebastian Morris, J. (1997). Traditional Native Culture and Resilience. *Research/Practice, 5*(1). Retrieved July 21, 2004, from http://education.umn.edu/carei/Reports/Rpractice/Spring97/traditional.htm

HeavyRunner, I. & Marshall, K. (2003). Miracle survivors: Promoting resilience in Indian students. *Tribal College Journal, 14*(4), 14-18.

Hetrick, C. & Martin, A. D. (1987). Developmental issues and their resolutions for gay and lesbian adolescents. *Journal of Homosexuality, 14*(1-2), 25-43.

Higher Education Research Institute. (2003). *Annual survey of freshmen.* Los Angeles: Author.

Horn, L., Peter, K., Rooney, K., & Malizio, A. G. (2002). *Profile of undergraduates in U.S. postsecondary institutions: 1999-2000.* Statistical Analysis Report (NCES 2002-168). Washington, DC: U.S. Department of Education, National Center for Education Statistics.

Hsia, J. & Peng, S. S. (1998). Academic achievement and performance. In L.C. Lee & N.W.S. Zane (Eds.), *Handbook of Asian American psychology.* Thousand Oaks, CA: Sage.

Huffman, T. E., Sill, M. L., & Brokenleg, M. (1986). College achievement among Sioux and White South Dakota students. *Journal of American Indian Education, 25*(2), 32-38.

Immerwahr, J. & Foleno, T. (May 2000, #00-2). *Great expectations: How the public and parents—White, African-American, and Hispanic—view higher education.* San Jose, CA: National Center for Public Policy and Higher Education.

Institute of International Education (2002). *Open doors: A report on international education exchange.* New York: Author.

Kaplan, C. N., & Colbs, S. L. (2000). Shattered pride: Resistance and intervention strategies in cases of sexual assault, relationship violence, and hate crimes against lesbian, gay, bisexual, and transgender students. In V.A. Walls & N. J. Evans (Eds.), *Towards acceptance: Sexual orientation issues on campus* (pp. 215-244). Lanham, MD: University Press of America.

Kim, B. S. K., Atkinson, D. R., & Yang, P. H. (1999). The Asian values scale: Development, factor analysis, validations, and reliability. *Journal of Counseling Psychology, 46,* 342-352.

Kraig, B. (1998). Faculty and staff mentors for LGBT students: Key responsibilities and requirements. In R. Sanlo (Ed), *Working with lesbian, gay, bisexual, and transgender college students: A handbook for faculty and administrators.* Westport, CT: Greenwood Press.

Leong, F. T. L. (1995). *Career development and vocational behavior of racial and ethnic minorities.* Hillsdale, NJ: Erlbaum.

Leong, F. T. L & Serafica, F. C. (1995). Career development of Asian Americans: A research area in need of a good theory. In F.T.L. Leong (Ed.), *Career development and vocational behavior of racial and ethnic minorities.* Mahwah, NJ: Erlbaum.

Louie, V. (2001). Parents' aspirations and investment: The role of social class in the educational experiences of 1.5- and second-generation Chinese Americans. *Harvard Educational Review, 71*(3), 438-75.

McEwen, M. K., Kodama, C. M., Alvarez, A. N., Lee, S., & Liang, C. T. H. (Eds). (2002). *Working with Asian American college students: New Directions for Student Services, No. 97.* San Francisco: Jossey Bass.

Murray, N. D. (1997). Welcome to the future: The millennial generation. *Journal of Career Planning and Employment, 57*(3), 36-40, 42.

National Center for Educational Statistics, Digest of Educational Statistics, 2002. (2003). NCES 2002-211. Washington, DC: U.S. Department of Education.

Padilla, R. V., Treviño, J., Gonzalez, K., & Treviño, J. (1997). Developing Local Models of Minority Student Success in College. *Journal of College Student Development, 38*(2), 125-135.

Reyhner, J. & Dodd, J. (1995, January). *Factors affecting the retention of American Indian and Alaska native students in higher education.* Paper presented at the Expanding Minority Opportunities: First Annual National Conference, Tempe, AZ. Retrieved February 5, 2005, from http://jan.ucc.nau.edu/~jar/Factors.html

Rhoads, R. A. (1997). Implications of the growing visibility of gay and bisexual male students on campus. *National Association of Student Personnel Administrators Journal, 34*(4), 275-286.

Rindone, P. (1988). Achievement motivation and academic achievement of Native American students. *Journal of American Indian Education, 28*(1), 1-8.

Rodriguez, A. L., Guido-DiBrito, F., Torres, V., & Talbot, D (2000). Latina college students: Issues and challenges for the 21st century, *National Association of Student Personnel Administrators Journal, 37*(3), 511-27.

Strauss W. & Howe, N. (2000). *Millennials rising: The next great generation.* New York: Vintage Books.

Strauss, W. & Howe, N. (2003). *Millennials go to College.* Great Falls, VA: American Association of Collegiate Registrars and Admissions Officers & LifeCourse Associates.

Suzuki, B. H. (2002). In M. K. McEwen, C. M. Kodama, A. N. Alvarez, S. Lee, & C. T. H. Liang (Eds.), *Working with Asian American college students: New Directions for Student Services, No. 97.* San Francisco: Jossey Bass.

Tapscott, D. (1997). *Growing up digital: The rise of the net generation.* New York: McGraw-Hill.

Tate, D. S., & Schwartz, C. L. (1993). Increasing the retention of American Indian students in professional programs in higher education. *Journal of American Indian Education, 33*(1), 21-26.

Trice, A. D. (2002). First semester college students' e-mail to parents. *College Student Journal, 36*(3), 327-34.

Upcraft, M. L., Gardner, J. N., & Associates. (1989). *The freshman year experience: Helping students survive and succeed in college.* San Francisco: Jossey-Bass.

U.S. Census Bureau. (2003). *United States Census 2000.* Washington, DC: U.S. Government Printing Office.

U.S. Department of Education, National Center for Education Statistics, Integrated Postsecondary Education Data System. (2004). *Enrollment in postsecondary institutions, fall 2001 and financial statistics, fiscal year 2001.* Washington, DC: Author. Retrieved February 3, 2005, from http://nces.ed.gov/pubs2004/2004155.pdf

Wall, V. A. & Evans, N. J. (2000). *Toward acceptance: Sexual orientation issues on campus.* Lanham, MD: University Press.

Wilgoren, J. (2000, May 4). College seen as essential. *The New York Times,* p. A-23.

Wong, L. & Mock, M. R. (1997). Asian American young adults. In E. Lee (Ed.). *Working with Asian Americans: A guide for clinicians.* New York: Guilford.

Yeh, C. J. & Huang, K. (1996). The collective nature of ethnic identity development among Asian-American college students. *Adolescence, 31,* 645-661.

Zhai, L. (2002). *Studying international students: Adjustment issues and social support.* (ERIC Document Reproduction Service No. ED474481)

Chapter 3
Understanding the New Relationship

Craig Ullom and Bill Faulkner

Entering the collegiate experience is an exciting and challenging milestone for students and parents alike. This passage from postadolescence to preadulthood is rich with opportunities for deepening the parent-child relationship and solidifying the foundation for managing future life events in the family. Beginning with the student, who is consumed with the developmental changes associated with moving to adulthood, and continuing with established mental models and evolving expectations on the part of students and parents, this transition to the collegiate experience can have significant impacts on the family relationship. Student affairs staff has an important role in working as a partner with students and parents to provide opportunities for ensuring student success and, at the same time, supporting a healthy and supportive family network that can help students prevail even in the toughest of times.

Developmental Tasks of PAPAs (Postadolescent Preadults)

Student Affairs professionals use a variety of models and theory-bases to explain and account for developmental issues faced by postadolescent preadults. Specifically, Arthur Chickering's and Linda Reisser's work (1993) on developmental tasks, or vectors, has been widely used and applied in a variety of contexts. Their theory proposes that college students move within these various vectors at different rates and levels of interaction among the other vectors (Chickering & Reisser, 1993). Although there has been some revision to Chickering's and Reisser's (1993) model over the years as well as increased efforts to test the model's salience to underrepresented populations, the basic foundations of the model remain intact to produce the seven vectors as follows:

1. Developing competence: The ability to cope effectively with and skill attainment to meet intellectual and personal challenges.

2. Moving through autonomy toward independence: The capacity to carry on life activities and solve problems without constant reassurance, assistance, and external approval.

3. Managing emotions: Awareness of and appropriate control of diverse emotional responses.

4. Establishing identity: Realizing an accurate understanding of self as well as a positive, stable self-image.

5. Developing mature interpersonal relationships: The ability to develop safe, healthy, and long-lasting relationships.

6. Developing Purpose: Clarifying and developing plans to reach educational, career, and life goals.

7. Developing integrity: Articulating personal values and creating a consistent belief system.

It should be recognized that students are entering college with different levels of competence in addressing the tasks associated with these vectors. In addition to one's competency level, the priorities attached to these tasks by students and their parents may be influenced by the immediacy of challenges and opportunities presented to the student as well as the interests of the student. Finally, it is important to recognize that students may be simultaneously expending energy on a variety of vectors but at different levels of intensity (Chickering & Reisser, 1993).

Additionally, recent research on the brain development of adolescents indicates that the physiological changes associated with brain growth may account for adolescent behaviors including emotional outbursts, reckless risk-taking, and a paucity of cognitive controls needed for mature behavior and decision making (Wallis, 2004). These findings contribute to the complexity of the developmental progression of students during the important transition to college life.

Mental Models and Expectations of the Collegiate Experience

Peter Senge refers to "Mental Models" as those embedded assumptions and generalizations that influence how we make meaning of the world around us from which we base our actions and responses (Senge, 1990, p. 8). These mental models are almost unconscious but drive our expectations of certain situations and contexts (Senge, 1990). Students and parents alike develop expectations of the college experience as well as expectations about how their relationship will change. These expectations are based on paradigms or mental models of how college should be or will be. The accumulation of impressions and information gathered over time that shape these mental models vary from person to person.

College-bound student impressions of college can be influenced by friends who are attending college, high school peers who plan to attend college, older siblings who are college students, and high school teachers and guidance counselors with whom they interact. Parents of college-bound students have a head start on constructing their mental models of college life based on their life experiences. For those parents who have attended or graduated from college, the memories of 30 years ago may still remain strong. The expectations of parents who did not attend college are formed to a large extent by impressions gathered from sources independent from personal experience. Similar to college-bound students, parents continue to construct their own mental models based on their own current experience, conversations with other parents and high school resource personnel, as well as experiences with having older children attend college.

A significant trend observed by student affairs professionals reflects a pervasive mental model demonstrated by parents of current college-aged youth. Modern parents are far more involved in their students' lives than in earlier generations. In the article, entitled "The Organization Kid" (Brooks, 2001), the author points out a clear trend on the part of parents to program their students' lives from an early age where nearly all activities are now planned and supervised by adults, as opposed to informal, self-organizing play which typified youth activities of earlier generations. Such a trend naturally continues into adolescence. Parents are also dealing with the mental models of Columbine and high-profile incidents at various colleges and universities, and therefore have greater expectations of the college to protect the health and well-being of their student. Also, recent research on the emerging college-age populations, sometimes referred to as millennials, points out that this generation of students demonstrates greater loyalty to their families and are not anxious to separate from their parents (Howe & Strauss, 2000). Please refer to chapter two for a more detailed description of this particular cohort research.

All of this equates to parents playing a greater role with their students in decisions of where to attend college and whether to remain. These decisions are influenced by access to information and media impressions that provide parents and their students with plentiful opportunities to fuel expectations about college. There are numerous college rating publications and trade books that directly target college-bound families. Some or the most commonly used include the Princeton Review, *U.S. News and World Report,* and *Peterson's Guide.* Films and television programs can also form powerful images that can influence one's perception of the collegiate experience.

With increasing marketing sophistication, colleges are providing information to college-bound families that contribute greatly to forming impressions and expectations. The process of reviewing literature, surfing websites, visiting college campuses, talking with college admissions officers, going to open houses, and completing applications provides families with considerable information to consider in making a college choice. The mix of anecdotal and personal experiences, media messages, and unprecedented access to information about colleges contributes to building mental models that are the foundation of expectations for the collegiate experience.

Being cognizant of the impact of these mental models is critical in understanding the relationship triad of the student, parents, and the college. An important role we have as student affairs professionals is to help parents and their students understand and make meaning of their mental models to ensure that there is mutual clarity and, ideally, an alignment of expectations that will support the transition to college life.

Parents need to understand how their behavior and attitudes are influenced by their mental models of college. Many times parents express perspectives on choices their student is considering based on their experiences as a college student in the '70s or early '80s. From time to time parents will be in conflict with one another based on differing expectations of what their student should or should not do in college. If this is frustrating for the parents, consider the level of frustration and confusion this causes the student.

Students are naturally forming their own expectations of the college experience and in some cases there is not consistency between their expectations and those of their parents. Perhaps the student places a lower value on the parent's perspective as compared to his or her peers or other significant adult influences that can result in discounting an important resource in the process of transitioning to college. Conversely, a student may place too high a value on parental expectations and by subjugating their personal views, can defer the developmental learning that occurs early in the college transition.

Both parents and students have multiple expectations of their college of choice. It is incumbent on the college to provide accurate and complete information to new-student families that is consistent with the reality of college life. Such transparency can facilitate the alignment of student and parent expectations with services and programs that are provided by the college.

Student affairs professionals can facilitate experiences that offer opportunities for mutual exploration and discussion of mental models and expectations early in the college transition process. By helping parents, students, and the college seek common ground, there can be a more complete and realistic understanding of the challenges and opportunities inherent in the college experience. Expectations can be clarified, questions can be addressed, fears can be managed, and relationships can be strengthened by providing opportunities for all partners to fully explore the collegiate transition. For

instance, student affairs professionals can assist parents through helpful publications and communications to understand their student's expectations for increased independence when they return home for holiday and semester breaks.

Potential Impact on the Family Relationship

The combination of a student's attainment of developmental competencies and the mental models and expectations of students and parents alike can impact the nature of relationships in the family as they collectively approach the transition to college life. The relationship between parents and between parents and the student (as well as other members of the family) can be strained as information is collected and analyzed, alternatives are considered, and decisions are made.

William Bridges suggests that the process of transition begins with an ending (Bridges, 2003). Something stops or something new begins. For a student, high school stops and the experience of college begins. It is important for students to understand that, regardless of prior success or status, they are now on a more level playing field with equally talented peers and have opportunities to launch a new identity in the context of a new community. For parents, day-to-day involvement with and perceived control over their child ends and a new phase of their lives as parents and partners begins.

Bridges (2003) goes on to say that the transition associated with change is the gradual, psychological reorientation process that happens inside of us as we adapt to the external change. Transition often results from a change but may also begin before the change actually takes place. Nancy Schlossberg refers to such transitions as "anticipatory" in which the event, such as beginning college, is predicted or at least foreseen (Schlossberg, 1995, cited in Evans, Forney, & Guido-DiBrito, 1998). Schlossberg and her associates further reveal that transitions encompass three distinct phases, namely, "moving in, moving through, and moving out" (p. 112).

Successful progression through these three phases depends on four primary factors: situational, self, support, and strategies. The situational factor involves the timing, ability to control, duration, and previous experience associated with the transition. Obviously, the more influence and/or familiarity one has with an impending transition, the more successful s/he will be in dealing with its requirements. Self as a factor refers to the psychological resources and personal characteristics that one brings to the transition. The support factor refers to the presence or absence of social support systems available to assist both students and parents through the transition. Finally, strategies refers to the abilities to cope with transitions. (Schlossberg et al., 1995, as cited in Evans et al., 1998).

It is this concept of transition that is important for parents, students, and the college to address especially in terms of its impact on our collective relationships. Applying Schlossberg's work, there are several factors specific to the evolving parent/student relationship that can affect transitions families may need to make as a student goes to college. The impact of these factors can be mitigated by appropriate and timely interventions by student affairs staff that can be of great assistance in helping students and their parents proceed through this period transition. These factors include:

1. Knowledge of the college culture (i.e., situation)

   Chaskes (1996) describes the acclimation to college life through an analogy of the student as an immigrant to a new country. The culture of college is quite different from high school and has changed considerably since mom and dad were students. For those parents who have not attended college, this new culture can be very daunting and confusing. It is important for students and parents to accelerate their learning curve to become conversant about the collegiate experience and culture in order to more completely understand what is happening and how to access resources in the process of transition to this new and complex environment.

2. What parents and students bring to the partnership (i.e., self)

Knowing and understanding one's mental models, expectations, and competencies are important steps in accomplishing successful transitions. By openly and honestly sharing these insights with one another, family members can develop a more complete awareness of each others' potential contribution to the partnership required for effectively navigating the collegiate experience.

3. Proximity to the student (i.e., support)

   Sometimes the distance between the parent's home and the student's college inhibits frequent visits and face-to-face interaction. Having a student move to an unfamiliar community can foster a level of concern, especially for the parents who are several hours away. When a student is living at home and involved in a variety of activities close to home, there is a great sense of awareness by parents of what is happening with their son or daughter. This changes when a student moves away to college, makes his/her own "home", and enjoys considerable autonomy from the watchful eyes of concerned parents.

   For some families, distance is viewed positively as it creates opportunities for building independence and autonomy. However, for other families the separation of long distances can contribute to anxieties about college life during the transition process.

4. How families stay connected (i.e., strategies)

   Some families are closer than others and the nature of this family connection can impact the transition to college life. Technology has helped many families maintain and enhance their connectivity. The use of cell phones, instant messaging, and e-mail make it very easy for students to be in virtually constant and immediate communication with parents. More personal strategies involve mutually agreed upon and preplanned visits to campus. Many institutions offer family weekends and sporting events that would facilitate such contacts. Family vacations can also be scheduled with the academic year in mind to ensure parents and students get reconnected. Finally, the time-honored "care package" that include notes, pictures, and audio/video recordings of missed family events can be a nice addition to the cookies and other goodies.

5. Advocacy, intervention, and control

   For years, responsible parents have exercised control over the life of their son or daughter. When not directly controlling aspects of their child's life, they have grown accustomed to intervening on behalf of their child taking actions that will protect and support opportunities for growth and development. Advocating a position to school officials and teachers that creates optimal conditions for their student is a common occurrence in our precollege educational system. Typically, parents, students, and college officials alike are challenged by the transitions associated with less parental control and fewer opportunities for intervention and advocacy.

As student affairs professionals, it is important to create opportunities for parents and students alike to address the transition issues associated with the changes in the family relationship, as well as the instrumental changes that they face in making preparation to attend college. Another variable to consider is the change caused by the introduction of a new partner in the life of a student: personnel from the college. This should be actively promoted as a positive development in that student affairs professionals can now provide another layer of support in times of crises, such as divorce, a death in the family, or a difficult financial situation. Such a change becomes the catalyst for modifying current roles of parenting and broadening the scope of resources, advocates, and partners that are provided by the college.

Common Issues and Questions Faced by the Parents of College-Bound Students

Developmental issues, mental models, changing family relationships, and transitions create a myriad of issues and questions that parents and students are eager to address. Helping parents and students identify and prioritize these issues and questions can provide a framework for conversation and exploration of strategies to effectively negotiate the changes and transitions to college life. Each family is different, having different experiences and expectations; therefore, it is important for a family to coconstruct a dialogue that can facilitate information exchange, promote understanding, and align expectations to minimize the adverse effects of transition.

Issues and Questions to Consider in College Selection

(a) Program: Does the college have what the student/parent wants as a program of study? What is the overall quality of educational and cocurricular experience?

(b) Price: Is the college affordable? Is aid sufficient to cover needs? What are the expected out of pocket expenses?

(c) Performance: Can the student perform to a level of satisfaction? How involved and connected can the student be at this college?

(d) Lifestyle: what are the options regarding such things as housing, dining, transportation, employment, personal finances, and insurance?

(e) Safety: Is the college environment safe? What can be done regarding crime prevention, personal safety, and property protection?

(f) Health and wellness: Is this a healthy campus? What services are provided to address physical and mental health? What is the extent of alcohol and other drug use?

(g) Value and prestige: Is the cost of college worth the quality of the experience and the achievement of outcomes by the student?

(h) Location: Is the campus urban or rural, in or out of state?

Implications for Our Work in Student Affairs

To be most effective in leveraging the relationship among parents, students, and the college, we must adopt a collaborative approach that defines the way in which we interact with one another. The notion of *in statu colleagarum*—or partners as a way of being (Ullom, 1997)—is a viable alternative to the age old in loco parentis philosophy that replaces the parent with the college rather than including parents as viable partners with college officials in the process of facilitating student success in college. It also speaks to the need for a potentially less contentious relationship based solely on contractual or legal parameters that has seemed to permeate American society. Adopting *in statu colleagarum* requires all partners to adjust their relationship paradigm with one another.

Adjustments Students Can Make

As students seek autonomy and self-reliance, they also need to accept self-responsibility for the choices they make in college. Parents should be considered by their student not as an advocate and intervener but rather as sounding board, supporter, and coach. College staff should be acknowledged by the student as viable resources available to support their total success in college.

Adjustments Parents Can Make

Parents should recognize and accept that their level of perceived control is less when a student is in college as compared to when the student was in high school, and should transition from the role as controller or manager to that of a coach. Parents should provide their student with space and time to make decisions while concurrently being informed and knowledgeable about the resource and opportunity-rich environment of the college. Parents can expand their family resource network by largely relinquishing the roles of advocacy and intervention to college personnel.

Adjustments College Officials Can Make

College officials should embrace parents as partners instead of isolating them as nuisances or worse, adversaries. Further, due to FERPA, the Health Insurance Portability and Accountability Act of 1996 (HIPPA), or other legislative restrictions, student affairs staff must create alternative opportunities for open and on-going communication with parents and let parents know of our commitment to work with them as partners to ensure the success of their student. College officials should recognize that they are not the sole experts in the life of students and that parents can be an essential asset to facilitating student development. Multiple contacts or points of entry for students can be created by the college so students and parents can easily access resources for success inside and outside of the classroom.

Specific Interventions for Student Affairs to Consider In Working With Parents of College Students

- Manage expectations by providing information and experiences to help students and parents construct mental models that are institutionally appropriate.

- Educate parents and students about predictable developmental changes that will occur in the college experience.

- Use media as a catalyst to explore reality in college and to present information that is more truthful and complete.

- Establish a reasonable expectations statement for the student-parent-college partnership and create opportunities for parents and students to generate their family-specific statement of expectations for their changing relationship.

- Provide avenues for on-going contact among partners such as newsletters, e-mail communications, phone trees, workshops, teleconferences, on-campus events, etc.

- Provide opportunities to help parents and their students find the "transition sweet spot" in which they can experience a level of comfort in their relationship through a process that includes being informed, communicating, and intervening appropriately when necessary.

- Create opportunities for parents and their student to intentionally address change and transition issues in their family.

- Create parent networks by helping parents of new students build connections with parents of upper-class students.

- Better understand parent and student issues and questions through assessment.

- Consider forming a parent task force to address strategies for working with parents in times of personal family crisis or campus-wide emergencies which might generate a high volume of parent contacts.

As practitioners in a values-laden profession, we are preoccupied with many tasks and issues. Perhaps one of the most significant tasks we face is the establishment of our own working relationship with students new to our institutions. This is important to us because it is the point of our life's work and we place a great value on our ability to interact with and assist students. While engaged in such an important endeavor, however, it is important for us to understand that we are relative newcomers to the lives of these individuals. Further it is important that we not ignore those that were part of these students' lives long before us (and will continue to be so long after us!), namely their parents. Student affairs practitioners are in a special position to facilitate the continued development of the parent-child relationship within the context of transitioning to college. By applying our sense of empathy and listening to the concerns each generation of parents express, we will continue to be effective in working with this important constituency.

Questions to Explore in Student Affairs

1. What structured programs or events currently exist within your division or institution that involve intentional outreach to parents (e.g., parent councils, family weekend, orientation sessions)?

2. How does or could your division set "reasonable expectations" for parents in regards to scope of services, standards of care, admissions criteria, compliance with FERPA, and other mandated legislation?

3. Are there specific times of the year staff receives a higher volume of parent questions or requests?

4. What are the common themes to such questions or requests (i.e. housing contracts, admissions status)?

5. What is the general reaction and/or attitude among student affairs staff when it receives persistent inquiries or requests from parents?

6. How can your division use technology to better inform parents, establish expectations, and gather feedback?

7. Does student affairs staff at your institution invest discussion time and/or training in regards to parent issues? If so, on what topics?

8. Based on the responses to the previous questions, what are some proactive strategies or approaches your division could use to address parent concerns and questions?

References

Bridges, W. (2003). *Managing transitions.* Cambridge, MA: Da Capo Press.

Brooks, D. (2001, April). The organization kid. *The Atlantic Monthly, 287*(4).

Chaskes, J. (1996). The first-year student as immigrant. *Journal of the Freshman Year Experience and Students in Transition, 8*(1), 79-81.

Chickering, A. W. & Reisser, L. (1993). *Education and identity.* San Francisco: Jossey Bass.

Evans, N. J., Forney, D. S., & Guido-DiBrito, F. (1998). *Student development in college: Theory, research, and practice.* San Francisco: Jossey Bass.

Howe, N. & Strauss, W. (2000). *Millennials rising: The next great generation.* New York: Vintage Books.

Senge, P. M. (1990). *The fifth discipline: The art and practice of the learning organization.* New York: Doubleday.

Ullom, C. (1997). *In statu collegarum: Developing successful partnerships which impact the student learning experience.* Presentation at the Institute of Higher Education, Division of Higher Education of the United Methodist Church, Nashville, TN.

Wallis, C. & Dell, K. (2004, May 10). What makes teens tick? *Time, 163*(19).

Chapter 4
Parents Orientation: Begin With the End in Mind

Jeanine A. Ward-Roof

A recent article by Jennifer Jacobson (2003) in *The Chronicle of Higher Education* found that "parental involvement in the college admissions process has increased in recent years"(p. A27). Not only are parents more involved in the admissions process, but they are also involved in their student's entire college experience. In response to the needs of today's parents, institutional staff and faculty are adapting their orientation programs to accommodate them. These programs can assist with the development of appropriate boundaries for these highly involved parents and provide a vehicle for candid discussions about campus expectations and realities. Comprehensive parent orientation programs provide an understanding of the campus culture and expectations to first-generation college parents who may be overwhelmed with the college selection and matriculation processes, and explain the unique features of the college to parents who have had a college experience or who have students at other institutions.

This chapter will focus on current practices colleges are using to serve this new parent population. In addition, this chapter will address why parents should attend orientation, detail components of a comprehensive orientation program, and make recommendations for colleagues who are creating or modifying an existing parent orientation program.

Current Literature

The first known orientation was held in 1888 at Boston University and has expanded exponentially since that date (Rentz, 1988). "With the transition from high school to college, orientation became the stepping stone for en loco parentis [sic] and facilitated the shift of the primary care giver role from the parent to the institution" (Johnson, 1998, p. 26). Although the exact beginning of parental inclusion in orientation programs is unknown, current practice suggests that

the present generation of students and orientation professionals find this process quite natural. Johnson (1998) found that orientation was one of the early times a student and parent were able to understand the roles an institution gained that were previously satisfied by parents.

Austin (2003) suggests that most parents were highly involved in their son's or daughter's high school experiences and that many students view the transition to college as the end of that involvement in all ways except financially; at the same time, parents seek continued involvement in their student's educational experience. Furthermore, she states that when institutional staff, faculty, and administrators develop means by which they can educate parents about separation processes, the parents are more willing to become an appropriate part of their son's or daughter's college experience.

Mullendore and Hatch (2000) state that the process of letting go is never completed, as it is long-term. No longer will just offering a parent orientation program satisfy the involvement wishes of today's parents; institutions must continue to partner with parents to ensure student success and appropriate parental involvement. Coburn and Treeger (1988) found that parents can experience a variety of feelings when their student departs for college, including expecting their role in childrearing to end and for their son or daughter to act like an adult, continuing their role as protectors of their immature son or daughter, or landing somewhere in between as they experience a combination of "anticipation and anxiety, a sense of loneliness and freedom, fantasy and reality" (p. 6).

The reality is that parents are highly influential in their sons' and daughters' education. Moreover, Mann (1998) found that well-informed parents are better able to assist their students with the understanding of the importance of campus resources. In addition,

Turrentine, Schnure, Ostroth, and Ward-Roof (2000) found that parents' beliefs can also help to shape the expectations students will have of college. Hatch (2000) concurs by stating that parents can also influence their sons' and daughters' satisfaction levels during college. All of this research concludes that parents are a vital part of new students' lives, and college faculty, staff and administrators should appropriately include them in the students' college experience.

Parent Orientation Surveys

An informal survey was conducted on a Southeastern college campus during a summer orientation program. The author notes that this survey included only a small number of parents, but at the same time it provides anecdotal information about some of the misinformation parents bring to orientation and some insights campus faculty, staff, and administrators can use to dispel these myths during orientation. One hundred parents were randomly selected to complete a survey during a summer orientation program and 37 families completed the survey. No demographic information was collected on the surveys; only the responses to the following questions:

1. As you complete orientation today, what are some myths (about any aspect of the campus) that you came to campus with that you find no longer true?

2. What motivated you to attend orientation?

3. What were you hoping to gain from the orientation program?

4. What insights did you gain from orientation?

The top two myths that resulted from the survey were: (a) no one will care about my son or daughter other than me, that the college environment is very impersonal; and (b) everyone in college drinks alcohol. The myths are representative of the concerns that parents of today's college students possess upon arrival on campus. The author recommends that these issues be addressed during parent orientation programs as they are indicators of what the concerns are from the families attending orientation.

The second question asked on the survey provides some insight on why parents attend orientation. The survey yielded responses that suggested parents wanted to better understand what was going to be expected of their son or daughter while in school, to learn how to provide support during this transitional period of their student's life, and to increase their knowledge about the school. The answers suggest that the parents are looking to make sure their son or daughter has chosen the correct institution, for ways they can stay involved, and to offer their son or daughter support as they make their transition to college life.

Another question on the survey asked what insights parents gained from orientation. The parents answered that they gleaned a better understanding of services and programs that were provided on campus; the financial, academic and social expectations of their family; and the fact that their son or daughter now had the responsibility to ask for assistance when it is needed.

Sandeen (2000) states that for traditional-aged students developing and implementing a quality orientation program for parents is an excellent way to influence the college experience. Upcraft and Farnsworth (1984) concluded that family and parent needs were one of four areas that should be addressed within campus orientation programs. Perigo and Upcraft (1989) concur by stating that assisting parents with their students' transition should be a common component of campus orientation programs. In addition, the Council for the Advancement of Standards (2003) suggests "student orientation program(s) must provide relevant orientation information and activities to the new students' primary support groups [e.g., parents . . .]" (p. 235). Ultimately, current literature supports the premise that parent orientation programs are a vital facet of the students' comprehensive orientation process.

An informal electronic survey was distributed to members of the National Orientation Directors Association (NODA) listserv and the Southern Association for College Student Affairs (SACSA) listserv participants. The author chose an electronic survey to minimize the burden of administration, to gather the orientation expertise of those who participate in the NODA listserv, and to gain a perspective from those who were in all types of educational positions; not just orientation. It should be noted that the response sample was limited in that it was small and dominated by institutions in the Southeast.

Common themes that emerged from the survey data were that institutional orientation programs expose parents to campus resources; make the experience as personal as possible; enable parents to meet and interact with campus administrators, faculty, and staff; offer opportunities to learn about transitions that will occur with the family; include open houses and receptions; teach the history and traditions of the institution; and discuss campus behavioral and academic expectations. Some examples of program activities that emerged from the survey can be found in Appendix C.

Developing a Parent Orientation Program

Parent orientation programs vary at each institution, however, there are steps that can be taken to develop an effective parent orientation program at any college. The first step in creating a comprehensive parent orientation program is to assess who the audience will be and what their needs consist of each year. Although the characteristics of most student populations do not significantly vary each year, the parents of those students could encompass a great deal of variety.

The second step in creating a comprehensive parent orientation program is to decide the duration of the programs that will be offered to the parents. Austin (2003) recommends providing orientation activities for parents beginning with the students' first interaction with the campus all the way through the end of the first year of enrollment, and she suggests that orientation is a perfect time to assist parents with understanding appropriate boundaries while including them in the educational process. Colleges can provide information to parents throughout the academic year, but the formal orientation program is usually 1 to 2 days in length.

The third step in developing a comprehensive parent orientation program is to determine the types of program offerings that need to be included and when the program will be offered (summer, fall, spring). Austin (2003) suggests that there are several issues that need

to be addressed when planning the parent orientation program, including timing (program length, time of year, day of the week); content of the program; facilitator and presenter selection and training; program costs; and method of evaluation. Issues that can be included in the program are the increase in student independence, challenges that parents face with the transition from high school to college, typical stress times of the academic year, and strategies to discuss the changes that will occur in the family life (Austin, 2003). Other facets of parent orientation programs can include introductions to campus resources; campus tours; discussion of academic and behavioral expectations; and information about campus traditions and history. Jacobs and With (2002) found that "clearly valuing parents and discussing development changes with them (parents) during orientation is very helpful. Parents who have an understanding of their own developmental changes would be presumably better equipped to assist students in their own transitions" (pp. 40-41).

Mullendore (2004) concurs and suggests that, in order to reduce parental anxiety, there is hierarchy to the creation of a parent orientation program. He suggests that programs should begin with sessions about the basic physiological needs, such as housing, food service, and financial issues. The next level should address safety needs, such as campus safety, health services, and alcohol and other drugs. The program should then progress to include the belonging needs, such as academic issues, advising, registration, career services, sorority and fraternity life, and religious groups. The last two levels are esteem needs of students (counseling, recreation, leadership, and involvement opportunities) and parental self-actualization, as parents learn how to stay involved with the college without being unnecessarily intrusive. These various levels can be offered during a one-time orientation program or throughout the first year of parents' experience on campus.

A sample parent orientation program schedule from Clemson University is provided in Appendix D. At Clemson University, parent orientation is the most comprehensive outreach program provided to parents. Other outreach methods include annual newsletters to all enrolled students mailed to their permanent address, Parents' Council activities, Family Weekend, and individual organization and office outreach to parents.

Recommendations

Based on the review of literature and years of orientation experience, the author offers the following recommendations for the creation of parent orientation programs:

1. Program goals should be aligned with the mission of the institution and the division where the program is organizationally located.

2. Faculty, staff, and administrators should assess the institutional parent population to best understand its demographics. Parents of today are more diverse than previous generations and parent programs cannot be based on traditional patterns of the past.

3. Orientation professionals should not only be aware of the developmental issues of students but also those of parents. Austin (2003) states that "knowing that the separation process is a mutual one, we do only half the job if we view the process solely through the adolescent lens" (p. 140).

4. Include current students and parents of current students in the parent orientation program. Parents are usually excited to learn from those who have experienced college life before them.

5. Use faculty, staff, and administrators who are going through the college transition process with their own students to assist with the delivery of the parent program.

6. Regardless of the size of the institution and the orientation program, keep the experience personal. Parents are comforted by the fact that students can find people who care about them and have time for them when emergencies arise.

7. Set boundaries for the parents. Be candid with them about what they can and cannot access at the institution. Provide them with examples of ways they can help their son or daughter solve problems for her/himself.

8. Develop and communicate to the parents how the college faculty and staff plan to interact with them on a long-term basis. Discuss where they can find information, who they can contact, and what to do if they have questions.

9. Address the tough campus issues. Discuss issues such as alcohol and other drugs, sexual assault, and campus safety.

10. Include unique aspects of the institution, academic expectations, and the components of campus life outside the classroom. Begin the program with basic parent and student needs and reinforce the academic and cocurricular resources available to them.

11. Provide parents with resource material in written form (such as a parent handbook). Include websites, important phone numbers, academic calendars, deadlines, stressful times for students, campus events, and other vital information.

12. Have participants evaluate the orientation program.

Conclusion

Campus faculty, staff, and administrators will ultimately have to decide the best way to plan parent orientation given the dynamics and demographics of their individual campus. This chapter provides some basic guidelines to understand the need for parent orientation, the importance of assessing parent demographics, and tools to design a comprehensive program. Parents are an integral part of today's college experience and if not included in the process appropriately, they may hinder the growth and development of their student. Implementing a quality, comprehensive parent orientation program suggests that the college values parental involvement and offers parents the means by which to understand their role on campus.

References

Austin, D. (2003). The role of the family influence on student services. In J. A. Ward-Roof & C. Hatch (Eds.), *Designing successful transitions: A guide for orienting students to college* (Monograph No. 13, 2nd ed.) (pp. 137-147). Columbia, SC: National Resource Center for The First-Year Experience and Students in Transition.

Coburn, K. L. & Treeger, M. L. (1988). *Letting go: A parents' guide to today's college experience.* Bethesda, MD: Adler & Adler.

Council for the Advancement of Standards. (2003). *The book of professional standards for higher education.* Washington, DC: Council for the Advancement of Standards in Higher Education.

Hatch, C. (2000). Parent and family orientation. In M. J. Fabich (Ed.), *Orientation planning manual* (pp. 39-44). Pullman, WA: National Orientation Directors Association.

Jacobs, B. C. & With, E. A. (2002). Orientation's role in addressing the development stages of parents. *Journal of College Orientation and Transition, 9*(2), 37-42.

Jacobson, J. (2003, July 18). Help Not Wanted. *The Chronicle of Higher Education, 49*(45), A27-A28.

Johnson, M. J. (1998). First-year orientation programs at four-year public institutions: A brief history. *Journal of College Orientation and Transition, 5*(2), 25-31.

Mann, B. A. (1998). Retention principles for new student orientation programs. *The Journal of College Orientation and Transition, 6*(1), 15-26.

Mullendore, R. H. & Hatch, C. (2000). *Helping your first-year college student succeed: A guide for parents.* Columbia, SC: National Resources for The First-Year Experience and Students in Transition.

Mullendore, R. (2004, February). *Mullendore's hierarchy of parent orientation.* Presentation to the national conference of the National Resource Center for The First-Year Experience and Students in Transition. Dallas, TX.

Perigo, D. J. & Upcraft, M. L. (1989). Orientation programs. In M. L. Upcraft and J. N. Gardner (Eds.), *The freshman year experience: Helping students survive and succeed in college.* San Francisco: Jossey-Bass.

Rentz, A. L. (1988). Orientation. In A. L. Rentz & G. L. Saddlemire (Eds.), *Student affairs functions in higher education* (pp. 203-255). Springfield, IL: Thomas.

Sandeen, C. A. (2000). Developing effective campus and community relationships. In M. J. Barr, M. K. Desler, and Associates (Eds.), *The handbook of student affairs administration* (pp. 377-392). San Francisco: Jossey-Bass.

Turrentine, C. G., Schnure, S. L., Ostroth, D. D., & Ward-Roof, J. A. (2000). The parent project: What parents want from the college experience. *NASPA Journal, 38*(1) 31-43.

Upcraft, M. L. & Farnsworth, W. M. (1984). Orientation programs and activities. In M. L. Upcraft (Ed.), *Orienting students to college: New Directions for Student Services, No. 25,* (pp. 27-38). San Francisco: Jossey-Bass.

Chapter 5
Channeling Parent Energy and Reaping the Benefits

Richard H. Mullendore and Leslie A. Banahan

Beyond orientation, colleges have additional opportunities to educate, involve, and embrace today's parents. Because many parents want to continue to be involved in the lives of their students, colleges should in an intentional, purposeful way provide structure and opportunities for that involvement. This chapter will assist institutions that want to develop or expand parent education and programming efforts. The authors will discuss planning parent/family weekends; publishing newsletters and other types of communication; developing a parent programs office and a parent/family association; creating a parent advisory council; and cultivating parents for fund-raising opportunities.

> Much of today's literature about parents and their college students encourages parents to just 'let go'. We believe 'letting go' is a long-term process that should never be completed. Instead we encourage parents and students to renegotiate their relationship based on the student's new status as a college student and an adult. (Mullendore & Hatch, 2000, p. 10)

Institutions should reach out to parents early in their student's college career and help them channel their energy into appropriate types of involvement. This chapter will provide the reader with multiple ideas for creating an inclusive environment for parents while respecting the developmental needs of both students and their parents.

"Administrators must balance their quest for parental involvement with the need for appropriate boundaries. Institutions must communicate with parents, and often remind them that their sons and daughters, and not the parents themselves, are enrolled" (Daniel, Evans, & Scott, 2001, p. 11). Seeking this balance provides staff with both opportunities and challenges. Certainly a quality, comprehensive, parent orientation program can begin the process of providing structure and boundaries for parent involvement, but orientation programs often provide an overwhelming amount of information and guidance in a short period of time, and even the best-intentioned parent will be challenged to remember every campus process, resource, and service when the information is needed, weeks, months, or even years later. And, not every parent attends orientation; colleges need to offer additional programs and types of communication to continue their dialogue with parents throughout the year. A parent/family weekend is a wonderful opportunity for parents to enhance their involvement with their student and the college, and serves as an official invitation for them to return to campus.

Parent/Family Weekends

Campus weekend programs for parents and family members can be as simple or elaborate as institutions wish to make them. Clearly defining the goal(s) for such a program is key to a successful event. An overarching goal may be to provide parents and family members an opportunity to connect with their student's college or university. Other goals might include providing information to parents about student development issues, campus services, and special academic programs for their students, such as study abroad, service learning curriculums, or support services for students experiencing academic difficulties; and providing parents opportunities to discuss with other parents issues and concerns they might have about their students' college experiences. Parents enjoy connecting with parents who have "been there, done that," so in addition to providing informal opportunities for parents to engage in discussion, parent panels with Q-and-A time are usually popular sessions. Student panels are also a popular offering and often provide lively and humorous discussions of campus programs, services, and events. Students definitely will "tell it like it is!" Typically, parent/family weekends have some element of fun and entertainment; concerts, lectures, local sightseeing tours, picnics, student talent shows, or athletic events give students and family members time together to experience the campus and local scenes. Some programs offer community service projects for parents and students to engage in as well as opportunities to attend classes or meet administrators and faculty in less formal settings. The campus weekend event is an appropriate time to conduct the annual parent association business meeting, introducing new parents to parent council members and various fund-raising aspects of the association.

Once goals of the weekend are defined and agreed upon, consideration of the timing of the weekend should be given careful thought. Fall weekends often have to compete with football schedules for campus facilities and hotel rooms, but for institutions without large football programs, it is possible to choose a date based on student development needs, trying to bring parents and/or family members to campus 6 to 10 weeks after the fall term has begun. Parents often request the weekend event coincide with a home football game, and for some institutions this might be possible, even desirable, but for those campuses with large, successful football programs, the logistics of planning a parent/family weekend around a home football game can be nightmarish or truly impossible. Finalizing the date as early as possible allows time for marketing the event to parents and their students before and during summer orientation programs, an important factor in the overall success of the parent/family weekend.

Many institutions offer more than one parent/family weekend, sponsoring a spring weekend, a mother/daughter or father/son weekend, a weekend for first generation college students and their parents/families, or another type of special event other than the traditional fall weekend. Some institutions specifically target their fall weekend for parents of first-year students, designing the programming to meet the needs and interests of new college parents, and then offering a spring weekend for all parents/families. This makes programming decisions easier and assures that there will be sessions of interest to all parents and families. Whatever the theme of the weekend, it is important to market the program to both parents and students, as well as faculty and staff.

A weekend program might include the following:

Friday afternoon
- registration
- faculty lectures/classes
- opening reception/welcome from the president
- banquet or dinner "on your own"
- student talent review/concert/comedian

Saturday
- fun run/walk or exercise time at campus recreation center
- breakfast with deans/administrators followed by parent/family association business meeting
- children's activities for siblings
- interest sessions (academic, student affairs, student/parent panels, etc.)
- picnic or luncheon with entertainment; service projects
- golf/tennis tournaments
- campus and community tours
- athletic events
- evening dinner or concert or free time

Sunday morning
- alumni/legacy brunch
- interdenominational worship service

Again, this is only a sample weekend schedule. Institutions that have sponsored parent weekends for many years may offer much more extensive programming, while colleges with limited resources or fairly new programs might offer fewer programming options to their parents and families.

Whatever the scope of the parents and families weekend, planning for the event is a wonderful and natural opportunity for collaboration among student affairs, academic affairs, athletics, development, auxiliary services, and alumni offices. A weekend planning committee with representatives from all of these areas, as well as officers from the parents association and interested students, can develop a dynamic and effective program for parents and families while allowing adequate free time for parents and students to visit, shop, and introduce new friends and roommates.

Costs are always a consideration in any programming effort, and parent/family weekends are no exception to budget challenges. Institutions must decide whether to charge one inclusive fee for the entire weekend or to itemize the costs of each weekend event and allow participants to "pick and pay" for various activities, sibling programs, entertainment events, and meal functions. The latter option gives attendees control over how much the weekend costs for their families, but requires more administrative work by the institution. An overhead or registration fee is usually included with either payment option.

Finally, a successful parent/family weekend is dependent on ongoing assessment efforts. Every aspect of the weekend, from the "save the date" mailing to the closing session, should be evaluated and reviewed as part of planning for the next year's event. Paper and pencil surveys can be included in registration packets and collected at the end of the weekend. Web-based surveys can also be used to gather opinions and impressions from weekend participants.

Communication with Parents

Technology has changed the manner and speed with which we communicate with one another in our culture, and this is made clear to us whenever we walk across our campuses, seeing student after student engaged in conversations on their cell phones. Often times, they're talking with a parent, as the baby-boomer and millennial generations are more connected with one another than any others in our collective memories (Tyre, 2003). Parents' close connection with their students naturally spills over to their students' colleges and universities. There is an expectation that there will be regular, ongoing communication, and that the communication will flow in both directions. Technology makes it easy for institutions to meet this expectation and provides multiple ways to both give and receive information.

In addition to printed publications such as parent newsletters, alumni magazines, campus newspapers, parent handbooks, and the old fashioned letter, institutions are using websites, electronic newsletters, listservs, and electronic mail "blasts" to engage parents in their students' college experiences. Content of parent newsletters should be carefully choreographed to highlight typical issues and concerns at the appropriate time of year: choosing on- or off-campus housing or theme residence halls; finding a summer internship; selecting a major; applying to graduate or professional schools; etc. Other articles could feature parent council members or parent/family association officers, parent fund-raising efforts, outstanding student philanthropies such as Dance Marathon or Relay for Life, or the parent programs office staff and services. Articles written by campus experts on the challenges students might be experiencing in and out of the classroom can provide parents with insight to important developmental and transitional issues their students might be experiencing. Topics for this type of article might include information on depression, test anxiety, time management, eating disorders, or drug and alcohol abuse, written by members of the counseling or health center staff. Another well-received topic is a humorous but informative article on students' weekend or holiday home visits as they struggle with and eventually embrace their new independence. (A sample of this type of article is included as Appendix E.) What is most important is that the editorial content of the newsletters be planned in an intentional and informed manner, conveying information relevant to parents at key times of the academic year.

Parent handbooks can provide a wealth of information to students' parents and families. In addition to printed handbooks, many colleges now offer their parent handbooks online as part of their parents' website. Some institutions incorporate information typically found in handbooks into glossy calendars featuring month-by-month student development issues and concerns as well as tips for what parents and family members can do to help their students overcome these developmental challenges. The counseling center at Texas State University–San Marcos (TSU–SM) publishes Seasons of Adjustment calendars for students' parents and a number of institutions now offer calendars based on the TSU–SM model.

Trinity University in Texas maintains Trinity's Parent Talk listserv as a means of connecting parents to parents, allowing them to engage with each other and the university. While student affairs staff members moderate the listserv, they try to refrain from posting responses to criticisms of their programs or services. Other than Friday Updates posted by the dean of students, Trinity staff is usually a silent observer of parent conversations and is able to gauge parent interests, concerns, and potential problems from parent comments (Kattner, 2004).

Electronic mail blasts are a convenient, efficient way to provide timely information to parents. Institutions can create class- and time-specific messages that are cued to be sent weekly, monthly, or bimonthly. Northeastern University's (Massachusetts) Inside Northeastern program delivers "Web-based tips and information to parents, helping them help their sons and daughters succeed during their first year at college" (Mercado & Brown, 2003, p. 6). Northeastern's messages are specifically designed for parents of first-year students and include financial issues and personal safety as topics. Parents may register for this free service by responding to an electronic mail invitation or by contacting Northeastern's Parents' Office. Institutions may choose to create this type of communication service using their campus resources, or there are a number of companies who market electronic mail blasts to higher education institutions.

Parent Programs Offices and Parent/Family Associations

To meet the expectations of today's college parents, institutions are designating individuals or offices to provide an array of services and programs for parents and families. The Carolina Parents' Office at the University of North Carolina (UNC) at Chapel Hill has a well-written mission statement:

- To encourage mutual understanding and to facilitate communication between parents and the University;

- To sponsor programs and services that meet the needs of parents and involve parents in the life of the University community, and

- To promote the development of the University and its students by supporting the Carolina Parents Fund.

(Hrdlicka, Duncan, Fisher, & Gibson, 2004, p. 30).

At the University of Virginia (UVA), the Parents Program was established in 1980 with the mission to enhance the student experience for all University of Virginia students. The Parents Committee that leads this important charter is comprised of talented and dedicated nonalumni parents from around the world. The Parents Program accomplishes its mission through fundraising efforts as well as proactive involvement within the university community. Each year, the Parents Committee allocates much-needed funds for academic and student life programs to a variety of university and student organizations. The Parents Committee also plays an important role in the University community, providing leadership as well as service. The Committee provides valuable resources to incoming parents and works to develop new initiatives and programs that will enhance the quality of the student experience at the university (http://www.uvaparents.org/about/intro.asp).

Both UNC and UVA have well-established offices devoted to parents and parent programs. A parent programs office serves as an easily identifiable source of information and referral for the myriad of questions and concerns parents have throughout an academic year. The office can provide campus and regional programs and written and electronic publications, and coordinate fund-raising events and campaigns with parents. The office should be staffed by persons familiar with student development theory as well as having a broad knowledge of the institution, parent transition issues, and fund-raising strategies. Strong oral and written communication skills are important, and since staff members in this type of office are often asked to make presentations, they should have public speaking experience and skills. Many parent orientation programs feature the director of parent programs during a session devoted to the student/

parent transition to college, which is an effective way to introduce new parents to the parent programs office, and its staff and services.

One issue that is certain to arise in the development of an office that serves parents is the funding of such an endeavor. With budget reductions and academic priorities as constants in higher education, how can a college justify expending scarce resources on an additional constituency? The authors believe that institutional acknowledgement of the current level of involvement of parents in the student experience is adequate justification to redirect some college funds to initially support the development of an office and/or parent program. These funds can easily be supplemented with funds from other sources to insure a quality program. Many colleges charge parents to attend orientation. Excess revenue from this charge can be allocated to ongoing parent programs, and some of the funds raised from parents each year can also be used to support the program. Developing a parent programs office provides an excellent opportunity for collaboration among the central administration, orientation, and development.

In addition to parent program offices, many colleges have established parent/family associations as a means to enhance communication with parents and to encourage constructive parental involvement with the institution. Many of today's parents are interested in joining and supporting a parent/family association if the mission of the association is clear and the benefits of membership are worthwhile. At some institutions, membership is free and automatic upon a student's matriculation, while other colleges charge either a one-time fee or annual membership dues to join the parent/family association.

Benefits accrued from membership may include newsletters (electronic or hard copy), access to websites and listservs, invitations to campus and recruiting events, local area merchant discounts, auto decals, college maps, T-shirts, etc.; however, the primary benefit should be ongoing access to information important to their student's college experience. The University of North Carolina at Chapel Hill, Syracuse University, Northeastern University, and North Carolina State

University all have well-established parent/family associations and could be good resources for those wanting to begin a program.

Parent Councils

Today, upper-level administrators must be responsive to many constituencies including students, faculty, staff, trustees, alumni, legislators, business and community leaders, and others in order to effectively manage the college milieu. Some administrators may ask, why should parents become a viable constituency as well? The reality is that parents have already made themselves viable by using their voices as consumers. They see the institution through an entirely different set of lenses than other constituencies, and they have clear expectations regarding the levels of service provided their students. Many colleges have developed parent councils to provide a formal voice for parents as well as to enhance college fund-raising efforts. A parent council can also be an effective mechanism for the college to channel parent issues and concerns or for the institution to use as a sounding board for ideas, issues, and policy formation.

Prior to the development of a parent council, parent committee, or parent advisory council, it is important that appropriate college officials agree on the mission and role (or roles) that the parents council will fulfill. Will the parent council be limited to a development function, or will the institution expand the mission to include other opportunities for involvement in the life of the college?

Developing a parent council provides a wonderful collaborative opportunity for student affairs and institutional development staff. For those student affairs divisions actually involved in fund-raising, parents can be a tremendous source of funds and/or contacts. The partnership with development can and should be a win-win if both divisions truly collaborate.

Student affairs serves all types of students: full-time, part-time, working, married, commuter, resident, advanced, remedial, traditional, nontraditional, underrepresented, underserved, and so on. Institutional advancement targets alumni, current donors, major donor prospects, planned giving prospects, opinion leaders, volunteers, advocates, sustaining sponsors, board members, and industry liaisons. Parents and families of current students make up the one set of stakeholders that often possess significant connections to both lists. It is incumbent upon higher education institutions to develop programs that effectively identify, move, manage, cultivate, and steward these families. This requires cooperative interaction, and unselfish collaboration (McInnis, 2001, p. 65).

If two divisions collaboratively develop a parent council, where should it report? This question is difficult to answer with any response other than, it depends. If the institution has a parent programs office, we believe the primary responsibility for the parent council should reside there. If not, then the locus of control will be dependent on resources and institutional politics and personalities. Based on the authors' experiences, the best true collaborations tend to occur when the program is located within the student affairs division.

Care should be exercised in the selection of parent council members. Most institutions require parent council members to be donors at a significant level to serve as an example for parent fund-raising activities. In the beginning, a considerable amount of research is necessary to determine which parents possess the resources to be asked to serve on the council. The council should be racially and geographically diverse, and carefully balanced among alumni and nonalumni, Greeks and non-Greeks, and so on. Nominations are often sought from existing council members, as they tend to know other parents who would be interested in serving. The council should consist of representatives from each of the classes, freshman through senior, and should meet at least twice a year.

Parent council members can be helpful in planning parent/family weekends, orientation programs, pre-college parties and other recruitment events, and retention and fund-raising activities. Parent councils are a great resource as an institutional sounding board, especially regarding sensitive, controversial, or financial issues. For example, parent council support for, or against, parental notification for student alcohol or other drug violations can be helpful. Parent council support of a new fee to finance a student union or recreational facility can sometimes tip the scale in favor of a project.

An important role for the parent council is to assist in raising private dollars for the institution. In 2003, the University of Virginia parent program raised more than $7 million (http://www.uvaparents.org/about/intro.asp). Not only should parent council members be actively engaged in fund-raising efforts, they should also have a strong voice in the allocation of money raised. Many colleges encourage faculty, staff, and student organizations to apply for parent/family association funds, and parent councils often make these allocation decisions. Parents typically favor projects and activities that directly and immediately impact students.

Funds can be raised in a variety of ways. Most common, of course, is telephone solicitation, which can occur in campus phone-banks with student callers or outsourced to companies that specialize in raising money for higher education institutions. The cost of outsourcing must be weighed against the benefits accrued. Mail solicitation is another method of fund-raising and information about giving opportunities can be included in parent newsletters or electronic communications. Using parents to solicit parents is the most powerful method of raising funds and seems to provide the greatest rate of success, especially for large gifts.

Many student affairs divisions support full- or part-time development officers, and parents are the logical primary constituency for student affairs. Alumni, business leaders, attorneys, and others are often "claimed" by academic departments, schools, or colleges, and are therefore off limits for student affairs development officers. If development is centralized and development staff are not attached to a specific unit within the institution, then it is important that student affairs clearly identify its needs and wishes and encourage the development office to solicit parents with an eye toward the needs of the student affairs division.

The authors have developed parent councils at three different institutions and have found the experience to be enjoyable and beneficial. We have also enjoyed considerable success in the parent fund-raising arena, with student affairs programs receiving tremendous financial benefits. In today's climate of limited resources, a successful parent council can make a huge impact on the student experience by providing expertise, support, and funds to meet special needs.

Concluding Thoughts

"By the time their children enter college, parents have become so invested emotionally in their success that they may not understand why it is so crucial that they remain outside the college gates" (Shapiro, 2002, p. A23). These words from a college president clearly resonate with today's student affairs administrators, and because parents often refuse to remain outside the gates, it is imperative that strategies, programs, and personnel be developed to respond to parental needs.

> Colleges may have no choice about whether they will deal with parents, but when it comes to *how* they interact with this important and influential group, they have many options. Each institution should develop goals and programs that engage parents appropriately and beneficially in the education of their sons and daughters. (Johnson, 2004, p. B11)

In this chapter, the authors have attempted to provide a framework for channeling the energy and influence of today's parents in a positive direction. The extent to which colleges are able to implement these programs will certainly be dependent on the size and type of institution and resources available, as well as the demographics of the student body. Parents may be a formidable constituency, but they can also be our strongest allies in our efforts to ensure students have challenging and successful educational experiences in higher education.

References

Daniel, B. V., Evans, S. G., & Scott, B. R. (2001). Understanding family involvement in the college experience today. In B. V. Daniel and B. R. Scott (Eds.), *Consumers, adversaries, and partners: Working with the families of undergraduates.* San Francisco: Jossey Bass.

Hrdlicka, S., Duncan, C., Fisher, D., & Gibson, L. (Eds.). (2003). *Carolina parents handbook.* Chapel Hill, NC: Division of Student Affairs, UNC-Chapel Hill.

Johnson, H. E. (2004). Educating parents about college life. *The Chronicle of Higher Education, 50*(18), B11.

Kattner, T. (Ed.). (2004). *National On-Campus Report, 32*(8), 1-2.

McInnis, D. (2001). Partnering with families through institutional advancement. In B. V. Daniel and B. R. Scott (Eds.), *Consumers, adversaries, and partners: Working with the families of undergraduates.* San Francisco: Jossey Bass.

Mercado, C. & Brown, S. (Eds.). (2003, Fall). Parentmatters. *Newsletter of the Northeastern University Parents Association,* 6.

Mullendore, R. H. & Hatch, C. (2000). *Helping your first-year college student succeed: A guide for parents.* Columbia SC: National Resource Center for the First-Year Experience and Students in Transition.

Shapiro, J. R. (2002, August 22). Keeping parents off campus. *The New York Times,* p. A23.

Tyre, P. (2002, March 25). Adultolescents. *Newsweek, CXLII*(12), 39-40.

Chapter 6
Legal Issues Regarding Partnering with Parents
Misunderstood Federal Laws and Potential Sources of Institutional Liability

John Wesley Lowery

Introduction

As a student affairs practitioner in residence life and judicial affairs, it was a fairly common occurrence for me to receive calls from parents requesting information about some problem or another that their students were encountering. Today, many student affairs administrators have reported a significant increase in the amount of parent-initiated contact with colleges and universities (Forbes, 2001). Unfortunately, these conversations follow an all too frequent path:

> Parent: "Hello, my son [or daughter] got in trouble recently."

> Student Affairs Professional: [Trying to remember who the student is and what trouble they might have gotten into . . .] "I'm sorry, but I can't talk to you about your student because education records are confidential under FERPA." [End of conversation]

The single most important legal issue for student affairs professionals to understand fully is the FERPA regulations which govern student education records. However, the key legal issues in working with parents do not end with FERPA. Student affairs professionals must also be aware of legal issues related to campus crime, HIPAA regulations, and finally, tort liability arising from failing to notify parents.

Understanding FERPA

The Family Educational Rights and Privacy Act was passed by Congress as part of the Educational Amendments of 1974. FERPA was an amendment to this larger piece of legislation sponsored by Senator James Buckley. Because FERPA was a floor amendment, the legislation was not considered through the traditional committee structure in the Senate (U.S. Department of Education, 2002). In introducing his legislation, Senator Buckley, who went on to serve on the Court of Appeals for the District of Columbia Circuit from 1985 until 2000, described various abuses in school records from an article that had appeared in *Parade Magazine* which was also printed in the *Congressional Record* at the conclusion of his remarks.

Senator Buckley (1974) warned:

> I speak of the right of privacy of millions of children in schools across our Nation whose school records are routinely made available to governmental and other busybodies, and the rights of their parents who are too often denied access to such information . . . These records contain not only test scores and medical reports, but also many so-called anecdotal comments which can haunt a child throughout his school years and beyond . . . But the issue of secret school records is only part of a larger problem of the violation of privacy and other rights of children and their parents that increasingly pervades our schools. (p. 13951)

Although the abuses in question were all taking place in K-12 education, the legislation was designed to apply equally to colleges and universities. Unfortunately, Senator Buckley's initial legislation was also very confusing and unclear. As a result, the legislation was amended significantly only a few months later. These amendments were designed "to address a number of ambiguities and concerns identified by the educational community, including parents, students, and institutions" (U.S. Department of Education, 2002, p. 1). The amendments to FERPA would not stop then, however. FERPA has been amended eight additional times since 1974 including several recent amendments directly related to parental access to records.

FERPA conferred upon parents, or eligible students, three primary rights related to their education records: (a) the right to inspect and review/right to access education records; (b) the right to challenge the content of education records; and (c) the right to consent to the disclosure of education records (34 C.F.R. §99).

In context of higher education, it is important to understand that, by definition, the rights under FERPA rest with the students, regardless of their age. This differs significantly from the K-12 context where the rights rest with parents until the student turns 18. Under FERPA, the records cover what the regulations refer to as "education records" and are defined very broadly to include all records which are (a) directly related to a student, and (b) maintained by an educational agency or institution, or by a party acting for the agency or institution (34 CFR §99.3).

There are various documents or records which are excluded from this definition including: (a) sole possession records; (b) records of a law enforcement unit; (c) employment records, except when a student is employed as a result of his or her student status; (d) certain medical records; and (e) alumni records (34 CFR §99.3). It is also valuable to note that the format in which records are created or stored does impact their status under FERPA. While records are broadly defined, a record must be created before information is protected under FERPA. For example, a conversation between a student and a student affairs professional is not protected under FERPA unless some record is created of that conversation.

FERPA and Parents

Generally under FERPA, written consent is required before a student's education records are released to a third party, including parents. In order to be valid, written consent must (a) specify the records that may be disclosed, (b) state the purpose of the disclosure, and (c) identify the party or class of parties to whom the disclosure may be made (34 CFR §99.30).

However, with the regulations for FERPA, there are several exceptions which can allow institutions to share information with parents from a student's education record without written consent. These releases are not mandatory under FERPA, but only allowed. Colleges and universities are free to develop policies within this framework for the release of information to parents. These exceptions include (a) release to the parents of a dependent student, (b) health and safety emergencies, (c) parental notification for alcohol and drug violations, and (d) release to the public of final results involving crimes of violence (34 CFR §99.31).

Release to the Parents of a Dependent Student

Under FERPA, an institution of higher education may release personally identifiable information from a student's education record without the student's consent to the student's parents, if the student is a dependent. The regulations allow disclosure "to parents . . . as defined in section 152 of the Internal Revenue Code of 1986" (34 CFR §99.31(a)(8)). The regulations define parents broadly to include, "a natural parent, a guardian, or an individual acting as a parent in the absence of a parent or a guardian" (34 CFR §99.3). Some institutions, most commonly small, private, residential colleges with traditional-aged populations, have taken the position that all students are assumed to be dependent students for the purposes of FERPA. However, the Family Policy Compliance Office (FPCO) in the U.S. Department of Education has indicated that if institutions make an affirmative or presumptive assumption about students' dependency status, then the assumption must be that students are independent of their parents for tax purposes. Only with some form of documentation can an institution determine a student's dependency status. Although the regulations do not specify the method for determining whether a student is a dependent, LeRoy Rooker, director of FPCO, discussed this issue in an interview published in *Synthesis*. Rooker advised:

> While FERPA does not offer guidance on what may be considered adequate documentation of a student's status as a dependent, we have said that a policy of documenting a student's

dependency status by requiring a parent seeking access to records to supply a copy of his or her most recent Federal income tax form is acceptable. (Lowery, 1998, p. 716)

However, Rooker also suggested another, perhaps simpler, process that institutions may wish to consider implementing in order to facilitate communication with parents. Institutions could request students to self-report their dependency status early in their academic careers. For example, an institution might request this information during an orientation. Rooker even suggested sample language for this statement:

> Under FERPA, the University may disclose to parents information from the education records of a student who is "dependent" under the Federal tax laws without the student's consent. Have you been claimed by your parents as a dependent for Federal tax purposes? (Lowery, 1998, p. 716)

This would remove the burden upon institutions from obtaining this documentation in many cases and simplify the process for determining students' dependency status. An alternative would be to seek written consent from students to release information to parents in advance of a particular incident, perhaps even during orientation.

Health and Safety Emergencies

The FERPA regulations also allow release of information from a student's education record without consent, including release to parents, in the case of a health and safety emergency. However, institutions must understand that the Department of Education strictly interprets this provision. In February 2004 testimony to the National Committee on Vital Health Statistics, Ellen Campbell, deputy director of the FPCO addressed the healthy and safety emergency exception.

> The FPCO has consistently interpreted this provision narrowly by limiting its application to a specific situation that presents imminent danger to students or other members of the community, or that requires an immediate need

for information in order to avert or diffuse serious threats to the safety or health of a student or other individuals . . . Any release must be narrowly tailored considering the immediacy or magnitude of the emergency and must be made only to parties who can address the specific emergency in question. (pp. 6-8)

From her comments, it is clear that FERPA is not a barrier when genuine emergencies occur, but institutions must carefully consider these situations on a case-by-case basis.

Parental Notification for Alcohol and Drug Violations

In 1998, Congress reauthorized the Higher Education Act of 1965 and amended FERPA to clearly allow institutions to notify the parents of students under the age of 21 when the institution determines that the student violated campus policy or laws governing the use of alcohol or other drugs. This amendment was introduced by Senator John Warner (R-VA). The amendment was a recommendation of a state-wide task force appointed by the Virginia attorney general after the alcohol-related deaths of five college students in the state. The task force recommended that institutions share information with parents about alcohol violations as a matter of policy and pushed for the amendment to FERPA (Reisburg, 1998). Senator Warner (1998) offered the following statement when introducing the amendment:

> As a parent, and indeed as a grandparent, I would want to know if my children were in the unfortunate position of being in violation of the law as it relates to alcohol and drugs while they were students at a college or university. I would want to step forward in a constructive way, as would other parents, to lend a hand and assistance to work with the faculty and administration of the college or university to help that student. But sometimes parents are not aware of these problems because of the provision as construed in FERPA. Our colleges and universities should be free to notify the parents of dependent students who have

violated the law relating to drugs and alcohol. (p. S7856)

The amendment was made from the floor of the Senate, but did not suffer from the ambiguities and confusion caused by the original legislation.

In 2000, the U.S. Department of Education issued regulations to implement this change to FERPA. The revised regulations explained that written consent from the student is not required if:

> The disclosure is to a parent of a student at an institution of postsecondary education regarding the student's violation of any Federal, State, or local law, or of any rule or policy of the institution, governing the use or possession of alcohol or a controlled substance if -
>
> (A) The institution determines that the student has committed a disciplinary violation with respect to that use or possession; and
>
> (B) The student is under the age of 21 at the time of the disclosure to the parent. (34 CFR §99.31(a)(15))

These provisions do not supercede any state law; for example, state law in California would prohibit release of this information. In the comments accompanying the release of the final rules, the U.S. Department of Education noted there was a low threshold that must be met for this information to be shared with parents:

> We note that an institution may make a determination under this exception without conducting any sort of disciplinary proceeding . . . Institutions may establish and follow their own procedures for making these types of determinations. The limited nature of this disclosure supports our interpretation that this exception does not require institutions to conduct any sort of formal disciplinary proceeding. This exception permits disclosures only to parents . . . Thus, we believe that Congress intended to make it easier for institutions to inform parents of drug and alcohol violations

by allowing the institution to release the information without conducting a formal disciplinary hearing. (Family Educational Rights and Privacy; Final Rule, 2000, p. 41863)

While the regulations allow for parental notification after only a "determination" that a violation was committed, most institutions with a policy or practice of parental notification typically make the notification only after the conclusion of disciplinary proceeding. Studies conducted in 2000 (Palmer, Lohman, Gehring, Carlson, & Garrett, 2001) and 2002 (Palmer, Lowery, Wilson, & Gehring, 2003) found that approximately half of the institutions responding to the survey had a policy or practice of parental notification. The authors noted that parental notification was more commonly found at private institutions than at public colleges and universities.

Release to the Public of Final Results Involving Crimes of Violence

The other significant change made to FERPA with the passage of the Higher Education Amendments of 1998 allowed the release of the final results of certain disciplinary hearings to the public. FERPA was amended to allow the public release of the final results of disciplinary proceedings when (a) the student is an alleged perpetrator of a crime of violence or nonforcible sex offense, and (b) with respect to the allegation made against him or her, the student has committed a violation of the institution's rules or policies (34 CFR §99.31 (a)(14)(i)).

The regulations define "final results" as:

> A decision or determination, made by an honor court or council, committee, commission, or other entity authorized to resolve disciplinary matters within the institution. The disclosure of final results must include only the name of the student, the violation committed, and any sanction imposed by the institution against the student. (34 CFR §99.3)

The regulations do not allow, however, the release of the names of any witness or victim without that student's written consent. The regulations provide an all-inclusive list of crimes of violence: arson, assault offenses, burglary, criminal homicide—manslaughter by negligence, criminal homicide—murder and non-negligent manslaughter, destruction/damage/vandalism of property, kidnapping/abduction, robbery, and forcible sex offenses. Release is allowed for nonforcible sexual offenses which are defined as statutory rape and incest (34 CFR §99.39).

While this provision was designed to allow for release to the public, institutions may also release information to a subset of the public, if all conditions are met. For example, if the parents of a student who was physically attacked by another student want to know the sanctions imposed against their son's attacker, FERPA would not prevent the release of that information, provided the student was found responsible through the campus' disciplinary process. This exception could also be used for release to the parents of the student who was found responsible. While release to the public is permissible under FERPA under the Jeanne Clery Disclosure of Campus Security Policy and Campus Crime Statistics Act, institutions of higher education must notify the alleged victims of sexual assault regarding the outcome of the campus disciplinary proceedings against their attackers—regardless of whether the accused student was found responsible.

FERPA and HIPAA

In 1996, Congress passed the Health Insurance Portability and Accountability Act. One of the most recognized provisions of HIPAA created federal privacy standards to protect patients' medical records and other health information provided to health care providers and took effect April 14, 2003. However, the consequences of the HIPAA privacy rule for institutions of higher education were lessened considerably by the final regulations issued by the Department of Health and Human Services in December 2000. The regulations exclude health records created or maintained by colleges and universities about students from the privacy rule. In the preamble accompanying the final regulations, it was noted:

> We have excluded education records covered by FERPA [from the HIPAA Privacy Rule] . . .

We followed this course because Congress specifically addressed how information in education records should be protected in FERPA. We have also excluded certain records, those described at 20 U.S.C. 1232g(a)(4)(B)(iv), from the definition of protected health information because FERPA also provided a specific structure for the maintenance of these records. These are records (1) of students who are 18 years or older or are attending post-secondary educational institutions, (2) maintained by a physician, psychiatrist, psychologist, or recognized professional or paraprofessional acting or assisting in that capacity, (3) that are made, maintained, or used only in connection with the provision of treatment to the student, and (4) that are not available to anyone, except a physician or appropriate professional reviewing the record as designated by the student. Because FERPA excludes these records from its protections only to the extent they are not available to anyone other than persons providing treatment to students, any use or disclosure of the record for other purposes, including providing access to the individual student who is the subject of the information, would turn the record into an education record. As education records, they would be subject to the protections of FERPA. (p. 82483)

Under these regulations, colleges and universities should follow the privacy protections of FERPA when dealing with health-related information about students. This does create considerable confusion about the status of students' health information. The American College Health Association (ACHA) has recommended that the FERPA exception to HIPAA be removed and that the Privacy Rule apply with equal force on campus (Knoblauch, 2004). While the National Committee on Vital and Health Statistics (NCVHS) stopped short of ACHA's recommendation, the NCVHS did urge the Department of Health and Human Services "to work with the U.S. Department of Education to clarify how the Privacy Rule and FERPA interact with respect to confidentiality of school health records, and where possible to harmonize these regulations and issue guidance" (Lumpkin, 2004).

FERPA's Bottom Line

It is vital for institutions and student affairs professionals to understand FERPA well. There are numerous avenues within the legislation described above which allow institutions to share information with parents, if the institution has decided to partner with parents in this way. Nancy Tribbensee, deputy general counsel for Arizona State, provided valuable advice regarding FERPA, "There's no need to work around it [FERPA]. There is nothing to prevent schools from taking appropriate action. FERPA isn't the obstacle" (Angelo, 2004). Institutions desiring to share information with parents freely are best advised to use some form of written consent or the dependency exception, rather than one of the other more restrictive exceptions discussed above.

Parents and Crime on Campus

In April 1986, Jeanne Clery was raped and murdered by another student at Lehigh University. After her death, her parents, Howard and Connie Clery began a crusade to require institutions to disclose information about crimes occurring on campus. They founded Security on Campus and successfully lobbied Congress to pass the Campus Security Act in 1990 which was subsequently renamed the Jeanne Clery Disclosure of Campus Security Policy and Campus Crime Statistics Act. Security on Campus:

> . . . believes that students and parents have the right to know about criminal activity on college and university campuses. Many schools are still not accurately reporting crime. Parents have the right to know about the academic and conduct failures of their students under age twenty-one. (Security on Campus, Inc., 2002)

Recent research (Warwick & Mansfield, 2003) suggested that parents are particularly concerned about safety and security on campus when evaluating institutions for their students to attend.

Under the Jeanne Clery Disclosure of Campus Security Policy and Campus Crime Statistics Act, institutions of higher education are required to prepare and distribute an annual security report to all current students and employees, and provide a summary to perspective students and employees. The annual security report must provide various policy statements related to campus security including:

- Procedures to report crimes;

- Policies for responding to these reports of crimes;

- Policies for making timely warning reports to the campus community;

- A list of the university officials to whom crimes should be reported.

- Security of and access to campus facilities;

- Arrest authority of campus police;

- Policies to encourage prompt reporting of crimes;

- Programs to inform about crime and take personal responsibility for safety;

- Policies related to campus sexual assault; and

- Programs on crime prevention.
  (34 CFR 668.46(b))

The annual security report must also include statistics for the previous three calendar years for crimes reported to campus security authorities and local police, including:

1. Criminal homicide:
   (a) Murder and nonnegligent manslaughter
   (b) Negligent manslaughter (beginning with 1999)

2. Sex offenses:
   (a) Forcible sex offenses
   (b) Nonforcible sex offenses

3. Robbery

4. Aggravated assault

5. Burglary

6. Motor vehicle theft

7. Arson (20 U.S.C. §1092(f)(1)(F)(i))

Institutions may either mail the annual security report to all students and employees or post the information to the Internet with certain restrictions.

Institutions of higher education are not required to share the information under the Jeanne Clery Disclosure of Campus Security Policy and Campus Crime Statistics Act with parents. However, given parents' acknowledged concern about crime on campus, institutions should carefully consider sharing this information specifically with parents to help address their concerns.

Tort Liability and Notifying Parents

One of emerging areas in higher education tort liability law are lawsuits against institutions of higher education after students commit suicide (Franke, 2004). In recent years lawsuits have gone to trial against the University of Iowa (*Jain v. Iowa,* 2000) and Ferrum College (*Schieszler v. Ferrum College,* 2002). The most highly publicized of these cases involves Elizabeth Shin's suicide by setting herself on fire at Massachusetts Institute of Technology (MIT) in 2001. Her parent's lawsuit against the university is currently pending (Farrell, 2002). In each of these cases, at least one of the parents' claims against the institution stemmed from the institution's failure to inform the parents about their students' mental issues and previous suicide attempts. Tribbensee warned, "Courts are moving toward imposing a duty on colleges and universities to share information with parents and families, if that information might prevent a suicide" (as cited in Angelo, 2004).

Franke (2004) discussed the many difficult issues which arise when considering whether to notify parents about students who have attempted to commit suicide or who have indicated an intention to harm themselves. Franke offered the following recommendation for institutions considering whether to notify parents in this difficult situation:

> From a legal standpoint, the safest course is to notify the family of a genuinely suicidal student unless previously known indicators, like a history of child abuse, suggest that parental notification would be harmful. Sometimes it just comes down to picking your lawsuit. A student's suit for invasion of privacy is, by most any reckoning,

preferable to a suit over a suicide. Be ready, however, for the unexpected. One college, after making the decision to contact the family of an international student, ran into the unanticipated difficulty that the overseas parents did not speak English. (p. B19)

However, the most important action which institutions of higher education must take, related to student suicide, is the development of clear protocol regarding how to respond to these situations when they arise, including both referral and treatment. Lake and Tribbensee (2002) described the Student Assistance Coordinating Committee at Arizona State which was developed to respond to students with behavioral and mental health problems, including suicide, as one model approach. Although the *Jain* (2000) court did not find a legal duty to notify parents of students committing suicide, the University of Iowa has also developed an extensive suicide attempt response protocol which includes parental notification (Baker, 2004).

Conclusion

As a number of the chapters in this book have noted, many institutions are experiencing a significant increase in parent-initiated contacts with the institution, and are seeking to develop partnerships with parents to help enhance student learning. This chapter has sought to eliminate many of the misconceptions about FERPA and other legal issues associated with communicating with parents about students. Consider this alternative script for a conversation with a parent who calls:

> Parent: "Hello, my son, Bill, got in trouble recently."
>
> Student Affairs Professional: [Trying to remember who the student is and what trouble they might have gotten into . . .] "Can you tell me what you know about the incident?"
>
> Parent: "Bill is a freshman and he was caught with alcohol in his residence hall."
>
> Student Affairs Professional: "Let me begin by telling you a little about how we address alcohol violations by students."

How this conversation continues would depend largely on institutional policy and philosophy. If Bill had been found responsible of an alcohol violation, the parental notification exception would allow for release of information about the incident to the parents. Furthermore, release may be allowed under the dependency exception to written consent under FERPA. Lastly, the institution could seek, or could have already sought, written consent to release information to parents. Institutions must also take into consideration how to respond to serious situations, especially those involving self-inflicted injury, in which the failure to inform parents may give rise to possible tort liability.

References

Angelo, J. M. (2004, January). Privacy or peril? *University Business, 7*, 39-42.

Baker, T. R. (2004, February). Suicide attempts and parental notification: Choices and consequences for administrators. Paper presented at the Association for Student Judicial Affairs Conference, Clearwater Beach, FL.

Buckley, J. (1974, May 9). Protection of the rights and privacy of parents and students. *Congressional Record, 120*, 13951-13956.

Campbell, E. (2004, February 19). Intersection of the Health Insurance Portability and Accountability Act of 1996 (HIPAA) and the Family Educational Rights and Privacy Act (FERPA): Testimony before the National Committee on Vital Health Statistics (NVVHS) Subcommittee on Privacy and Confidentiality.

Family Educational Rights and Privacy Act, 20 U.S.C. §1232g (1974).

Family Educational Rights and Privacy Act of 1974, 20 U.S.C. §1232g; 34 C.F.R. §99 (2004).

Family Educational Rights and Privacy Act, 20 U.S.C. §1232g (1974). Family Educational Rights and Privacy; Final Rule. (2000). *Federal Register, 65*, 41851-41863.

Farrell, E. F. (2002, May 24). A suicide and its aftermath. *Chronicle of Higher Education*, p. A37.

Forbes, K. J. (2001, September/October). Students and their parents: Where do campuses fit in? *About Campus, 6*, 11-17.

Franke, A. H. (2004, June 25). When students kill themselves, colleges may get the blame. *Chronicle of Higher Education*, pp. B18-B19.

Higher Education Amendments of 1998, Pub. L. No. 105-244, 112 Stat. 1581 (1998).

Jain v. Iowa, 617 N.W.2d 293 (Iowa, 2000).

Jeanne Clery Disclosure of Campus Security Policy and Campus Crime Statistics Act, 20 U.S.C. §1092(f); 34 C.F.R. §668.46 (2004).

Jeanne Clery Disclosure of Campus Security Policy and Campus Crime Statistics Act, 20 U.S.C. §1092(f) (1990).

Knoblauch, E. (2004, February 19). American College Health Association (ACHA) Statement on the Health Insurance Portability and Accountability Act of 1996 (HIPAA) Privacy Rule: Testimony before the National Committee on Vital Health Statistics (NVVHS) Subcommittee on Privacy and Confidentiality.

Lake, P., & Tribbensee, N. (2002). The emerging crisis of college student suicide: Law and policy responses to serious forms of self-inflicted injury. *Stetson Law Review, 32*, 125-157.

Lowery, J. W. (1998, Fall). LeRoy Rooker on FERPA as a defender of education and privacy rights on today's college campus. *Synthesis: Law and Policy in Higher Education, 10*, 716-717, 731-732.

Lumpkin, J. R. (2004). Letter to the Secretary— Recommendations on the effect of the privacy rule in schools. Retrieved July 1, 2004, from U.S. Department of Health and Human Services, National Committee on Vital and Health Statistics: http://www.ncvhs.hhs.gov/040617l2.htm.

Palmer, C. J., Lohman, G., Gehring, D. D., Carlson, S., & Garrett, O. (2001). Parental notification: A new strategy to reduce alcohol abuse on campus. *NASPA Journal, 38,* 372-385.

Palmer, C. J., Lowery, J. W., Wilson, M. E., & Gehring, D. D. (2003). Parental notification policies, practices, and impacts in 2000 and 2002. *Journal of College and University Student Housing, 31*(2), 3-6.

Reisberg, L. (1998, December 4). When a student drinks illegally, should colleges call mom and dad? *Chronicle of Higher Education,* p. A39.

Schieszler v. Ferrum College, 233 F. Supp. 2d 796 (W. D. Va. 2002).

Security on Campus, Inc. (2002). *About Security on Campus, Inc.* Retrieved July 2, 2004, from http://www.securityoncampus.org/aboutsoc/index.html.

Standards for Privacy of Individually Identifiable Health Information; Final Rule. (2000, December 28). *Federal Register, 65,* 82461-82510.

U.S. Department of Education, Family Policy Compliance Office. (2002). *Legislative history of major FERPA provisions.* Retrieved July 2, 2004, from http://www.ed.gov/policy/gen/guid/fpco/pdf/ferpaleghistory.pdf.

Warner, J. W. (1998). Statement introducing Amendment 3117 to the Higher Education Amendments of 1998. 144 Cong. Rec. S7856-S7857.

Warwick, J. & Mansfield, P. M. (2003.) Perceived risk in college selection: Differences in evaluative criteria used by students and parents. *Journal of Marketing for Higher Education, 13,* 101-125.

Chapter 7
Managing Parent Expectations: My How Times Have Changed

Michael L. Jackson and Sheila Murphy

A parent told one of us that she calls her daughter almost every day to ask her how she is doing, to check on how she is handling her homework, and to make sure her assignments are done before she goes out on the weekends. My, how times have changed!

The purpose of this chapter is to review the changes in higher education over the past 30 years as they relate to parental involvement in undergraduate student life, to illuminate the cultural and economic factors that have given rise to these changes, to provide an overview of selected institutional responses to parents as constituents, and to recommend best practices for student affairs practitioners to follow to ensure a mutually beneficial relationship with parents of traditional-age undergraduate students.

Conversations about the expectations of the current generation of college and university student parents have changed in the last several decades. Presidents, provosts, deans of academic programs and student affairs leaders and professionals at all levels are now more engaged in working directly with parents to better manage their involvement with institutions. Such challenges were almost unheard of 30 years ago.

This new trend has its roots in an interesting and complex blend of societal, economic, and cultural forces. In hardly more than a generation's time, parent-child relationships have evolved into partnerships and the cost of higher education has increased at a level disproportionate to the consumer price index. Further, the consumer culture, with its rallying cry of "customer service" has become a defining force in most transactions, including the university-student relationship.

Many practitioners in leadership roles in colleges and universities today were on campus as students in the late 1960s and early 1970s. Most can recall an unspoken code that ruled the parent-child discourse: Be interested and committed to your child's education, demonstrate your interest through financial support,

and leave the rest up to the student. For many parents, Labor Day weekend meant the annual pilgrimage to campus, helping a son or daughter move, taking a quick tour of the campus, and getting back on the road to beat the traffic home and ensure that no more than one day of work was missed. Parents may have returned for a visit or two during their child's college career and again for graduation. But only in the most dire of circumstances would the parent violate the fundamental tenet of the code: no contact with the university on the student's behalf. Students valued the responsibility to speak for themselves and solve their own problems, and were uniformly mortified by any suggestion of an alternative arrangement. They wanted their parents to support them in their emerging independence and only get involved if they asked for their help.

Jump forward 30 years. Many parents not only take precollege tours with their children and explore higher education options on the internet, but they also enroll their students in SAT and college preparatory courses, hire college placement professionals to assist with the application process, and attend on-campus orientation programs with their students. They listen very attentively to presentations about academic programs, cocurricular activities, housing and food options, financial aid, safety, and emergency protocols. Many parents move their student into their freshman residences and stick around for a couple of days to help them set up their room and take care of new student administrative work, such as paying bills, setting up computers, and opening checking accounts. In some extreme cases, parents attend the first meetings organized by resident assistants to help new students get to know each other and build community. It appears to many student affairs practitioners that the on-going involvements of today's parents in their student's college education have intensified, and now include trying to take care of routine campus business for their student rather than giving to the son or daughter the primary responsibility for such matters. In subtle and overt ways, there is a recognizable effort to manage the student's experience in ways that worked when the student was at home. Electronic communication makes it easy. Parent-to-parent advice on many campuses includes the suggestion to buy the "Family Plan" cell phone service and link together the whole family for daily chats and updates that resemble time around the dining room table. Instant Messenger (IM-ing) communication seems inevitable between students and working parents, many of whom spend the better part of their day in front of a computer. IM-ing mirrors the experience of going into the next room to ask a simple, logistical question; but instead of "Where are my shoes?", it is "When is your plane landing?", or "Did you mail my tax forms?", or "Do you think I should take more French or start in Italian?"

Parents want to make sure they approve of the environment in which their student will be living. They need to see for themselves how their student is going to get the support and guidance they need to be successful. They want to ensure that their student is going to get the most out of the collegiate experience, because the current generation of parents have invested a lot of emotional energy, love, and money in getting their student to this point in her/his life. An example of how these parental needs are expressed is provided in the words of Joel Garreau, a Washington, DC-based writer and father of an freshman incoming freshman at George Washington University.

> Anything that combines love and money gets my attention. Here's what I wanted to know when we were shopping for a school: Will she be around interesting students whose life experiences will help her learn? Will anyone pay attention to her if she really needs help? How can I calculate the return on my investment? Suppose I offered her $150,000 and said, "Travel around the world and figure out who you are"—would that be a better use of my money? (personal communication, July 2002)

Some parents attempt to live their student's college experience. For example, one mother of a student at a southern university drove to campus to distribute her son's resume at an on-campus career fair because she wasn't confident that he intended to get there on his own. In another situation, a parent unconsciously used the plural pronoun "we" in all conversations relating to the student/college relationship, such as: "We feel we have to question the final grade in this course because the exam required knowledge of material that was not specified on the syllabus." In addition, there is the cadre of specialists with whom the college may be asked to interact in establishing the student's needs and possible institutional interventions, including the therapist, the learning disabilities specialist, the lawyer, college counselor, and others. Is this reasonable? How do we make sense of the shift in parent behavior and expectations in a way that allows colleges and universities to do what they do best, educate students?

Our sense is that parents are redefining the relationship between the institution and the student in ways that none of us yet understand because the behavior we are seeing is so recent. We are just beginning to recognize that the student's relationship with her college is changing, and we will not fully know the impact of this change until it has been studied more carefully and discussed at an institutional and national level. What we have to figure out is how to work effectively with parents while helping students develop their own sense of self-efficacy, voice, and independence, within the context of their relationships with their parents.

College and university leaders must also understand that today's parents want to play an important role in the continuing developmental and educational process of students enrolled in their institutions. For example, in a recent publication about how the learning environment must change to meet the needs of today's college students, the authors of *Learning Reconsidered: A Campus-Wide Focus on the Student Experience* (National Association of Student Personnel Administrators & American College Personnel Association, 2004) describe how the educational environment and teaching strategies of institutions of higher education must evolve to meet student needs. They describe how colleges and universities must develop a more transformative approach to learning:

In the transformative educational paradigm, the purpose of educational involvement is the evolution of multidimensional identity, including but not limited to cognitive, affective, behavioral and spiritual development. Therefore learning, as it has historically been understood, is included in a much larger context that requires consideration of what students know, who they are, what their values and behavior patterns are, and how they see themselves contributing to and participating in the world in which they live. (p.9)

These ideas have clear implications for the role of parents as campus partners in the education of their students. They are closely involved in the learning process and they influence the educational and developmental choices of their students as they encourage and/or prod them to explore courses, majors, minors, cocurricular activities, internships, community services, career, and postundergraduate education. Student affairs professionals must not ignore this dynamic. Effective strategies must be developed to keep them engaged in the educational process in positive ways or they could be a hindrance to what institutions want students to accomplish while on campus.

How Much Involvement Is Enough?

Parental concern and involvement are not new phenomena in higher education. Perhaps the significance of the change is a matter of degree. How much parental involvement is enough? How much is too much? What happens when the institution sends mixed signals to parents about the role they are invited to play in the life of the college or university? What are reasonable expectations for parents to have of the university? And, conversely, what expectations are reasonable for the college or university to have of parents? There are no easy answers to these questions. Responses will be found within the context of each institution and the kinds of students and families that take advantage of its programs. In other words, what kind of clientele are you working with and what are their expectations?

In a study conducted in 2000, Public Agenda, a Washington, DC-based public policy think tank, studied public perceptions of higher education, and included in their analysis differences in expectations among racial groups. The findings, summarized in *Great Expectations: How the Public and Parents— White, African American and Hispanic—View Higher Education* (Immerwahr & Foleno, 2000) confirm the widespread belief that a college education is the essential gateway to the middle class. More interesting, however, is the widespread public belief that colleges have a responsibility that extends far beyond the credential of a degree and includes personal growth, the development of skills for professional and personal success, and a broadened perspective on the world. This not only provides more information about what parents think, but also what they expect the college or university their student attends to do for them. Parents stay more involved in their student's higher educational experience to try to ensure that these expected outcomes become a reality.

New Parent Roles and Financial Aid

Parents in the above-cited study embrace the philosophy that no qualified and interested student should be denied the opportunity to attend college for financial reasons. At the same time, the study shows that parents, and the public in general, believe that anyone who really wants a college education can figure out a way to attend, despite the cost. Parents acknowledge that they are worried about the cost, but at the same time they are convinced that they will somehow figure out a way to pay for it (Immerwahr & Foleno, 2000, p. 21).

These finding are consistent with the dynamic that many student affairs practitioners encounter on campus. Financial-aid officers are routinely approached with requests to add on to established financial-aid packages, to alter the grant/loan ratio, and to "negotiate" the package. "A school has the opportunity to express how much they want a student by the composition of the aid package," says a suburban New York father of two daughters in private colleges in the East (personal communication, May 2001).

Would you bid the asking price on a house? Would you pay the sticker price for a car? Negotiation is the essential business skill of the 21st century and college costs are no different. Of course the schools *must* put these packages together expecting some push back. It is the way the world works these days. (personal communication, May 2001)

"Not exactly," says Jim Miller, (personal communication, February 2004) who in 2001 was appointed dean of admission and student aid at Bowdoin College in Brunswick, Maine. According to Miller, the often misunderstood postacceptance "dance" between the family and the college has its roots in the "courtship ritual" that has been in play for, in many cases, up to 3 years:

> I'd be reluctant to say that most families consider the aid package as received to be merely the opening bid. Rather, I think the tension results from the family's hope that the package will be an expression of the college's love and affection, rather than an objective calculation of one's ability to purchase an admittedly quite expensive opportunity. (personal communication, February 2004)

Adding to the complexity, according to Miller, is the fact that awarding financial aid is rather an imprecise science. A student who gets five acceptance letters is likely to receive five financial-aid packages, all different, some significantly so.

> This range of responses is what contributes to the parental sense that financial aid is some sort of game in which only the college really understands the rules and the strategy. Parents don't want to feel "taken." They need to feel that they have tried to invest their resources wisely. (personal communication, February 2004)

The 1990 Justice Department ruling (Jaschik, 1990), which enacted antitrust legislation and now forbids colleges from sharing information about financial-aid awards, is a significant factor in changing parental expectations about the aid process. Although a set of highly selective schools was named in the highly

publicized suit, the ripple effects have been significant. Parents might reasonably expect some congruence among the aid packages they receive from similarly priced schools, but the schools themselves are denied the opportunity to coordinate their responses, a factor which adds to the confusion.

The *Great Expectations* study further indicates that the public emphasizes the responsibility of college students to contribute to their own successes. While acknowledging the role of the university in assisting students in need, the study's findings indicate that the public wants schools to focus on helping those who help themselves by contributing to the financing of their education and taking advantage of the educational opportunities available to them. According to the study, the public's expectations of higher education and the learning-centered agenda that has for the last decade informed the organization and delivery of most student affairs programs are well aligned.

New Parent Roles and New Goals For a College Degree

As recently as 1993, participants in an earlier version of the study, *The Price of Admission: The Growing Importance of Higher Education* (Immewahr, 1998), drew a linear connection between a college degree and a set of job-related skills (p. 9). By the 1998 update of the study, the public had begun to acknowledge "the less tangible qualities bestowed by higher education over and above the degree itself" that the degree itself was not the only quality recognized as valuable. These less tangible qualities are familiar to student affairs professionals and include: (a) a sense of maturity and how to manage on their own; (b) an ability to get along with people different from themselves; (c) an improved ability to solve problems and think analytically; (d) technological competency; (e) excellent writing and speaking skills; and (f) recognition of the responsibilities of citizenship, including voting and volunteering. These skills for both personal and professional success, needed for the citizen of the 21st century, are remarkably similar in scope and content to the learning goals imbedded into the programs and services of many student affairs divisions around the country.

How Should Schools Respond to the Dynamics We Are Managing?

Whose responsibility is it to address the concerns of parents, while keeping in mind that the job of student affairs professionals is to help create an integrated learning experience that helps students reach their educational, personal, and professional aspirations? We do so by supporting students in their development: intellectual, moral, ethical, social, cultural, emotional, and physical. How can we help students become independent learners in the context of seemingly over-involved parents? And, are parents really too involved in their students' college education?

Again, there are no easy answers to these questions. It is clear, however, that student affairs professionals must work cooperatively with other institutional leaders and faculty to ensure that students are their first priority, no matter what pressures are exerted by parents to influence the educational process. This work, particularly for the last 30 years, has been done in the context of fostering independence and encouraging students to take personal responsibility for their education when they first set foot on campus. The current trend of increasing parental involvement in the education of students in college has become a complicated process and one that will not give way to easy resolution.

Parent Programming on Campuses Today

Hardly more than a thinly disguised extension of the development office's annual fund not so many years ago, today the parent council (or parent association, parent league, or family association) has become a standard feature on hundreds of campuses around the country. The very existence of these programs signals an acknowledgement of parents as a bona fide constituency, entitled to recognition, services, and an extensive array of membership benefits ranging from warehouse club discounts to affinity credit cards. According to an article by Eric Hoover (2004) in *The Chronicle of*

Higher Education, parent programs are a standard feature on campuses all over the country. Many of these programs share common purposes and attempt to keep parents informed and engaged with the college or university, and by extension, with their student. Several examples from college and university websites appear in the model programs in Appendix A. We must be aware of the trends and develop strategies to help our schools successfully work with this important constituency. The following are some recommendations to consider when examining how well your institution is responding to the new role of parents in the education of their students.

Recommendations and Other Considerations for Student Affairs Professionals

- Create a clearly articulated position that frames the parent-institution relationship. Success in this endeavor will help contextualize all efforts to work with parents in productive and helpful ways.

- Keep sight of your paramount objective: Providing an excellent learning experience for students. Managing parental expectations and institutional involvements should be evaluated against this overarching goal. Student affairs professionals need to determine if an initiative to increase parental involvement in their institution will enhance the student experience.

- Turn the clear, developmental contradictions presented through parental involvement in undergraduate life into occasions for thoughtful discussions with parents. Issues that might be discussed with parents include: (a) institutional responses to student use of alcohol and other drugs; (b) parental expectations about their student's academic performance and how they can help prevent academic dishonesty; (c) a review of the expectations parents may have of the institution and those the institution has of parents and students; and (d) guiding parents through discussions they should have with their student about expectations and ways in which their involvement might actually be useful, and those times in which it might be best for them to keep their distance.

- Develop a personal understanding of how parents are now involving themselves in the lives of students on your campuses. Baby-boomer parents, like their millennial offspring, are a much-studied generation. Their behavior relative to their student's experiences in college is entirely consistent with what we should know about them. This is the first generation of students, and many parents, to incorporate technology into their day-to-day lives. Expect them to conduct independent research on many of your school's websites to compare the fine points of language requirements, study-abroad offerings, and law school admission records. As these parents raised this highly scheduled, programmed, and structured generation now on our campuses, it should come as no surprise that they are taking advantage of both the nation's consumer sensibilities and technological advances to "manage" their student's experiences away from home.

- Work with institutional leaders (the president, provost, dean of the college, and other administrative and academic leaders) to develop a common understanding of how the institution will approach interacting with, and responding to, parents during the time of their student's matriculation. Be explicit and intentional in developing best practices for parental involvement.

- Develop an institutional philosophy on working with parents that can be discussed on a campus-wide basis by faculty, staff, trustees, and other significant constituencies to ensure the institution is operating in a consistent manner.

- Create a well-crafted internal institutional position that can help the college or university persuade parents that: (a) their concerns are important, but not uncommon; (b) the institution hears concerns like theirs routinely; and (c) the institution has a track record of developing thoughtful policies and practices that have been successful in meeting the needs of those who came before them and are likely to be successful in also assisting their students.

- Develop "talking points" for residence life staff, including student staff, for use when discussing housing-related concerns with parents. It makes sense

that parents would assert a high level of hands-on involvement when discussing a student's need for appropriate shelter: They know how large their child's room is at home, how many electrical outlets it has, and how many family members are expected to live in it! Discuss in preservice and in-service training the institutional message about accommodations, the expectation for civility among roommates, and that situations that often appear problematic to parents in fact turn out to be successful arrangements in the eyes of students. Encourage lower-level staff to offer opportunities to discuss concerns with upper-level administrators at the college, a strategy which often has the effect of putting a superficial issue to rest.

- Educate staff that most often interact with parents about the new trends in parental behavior in higher education settings to ensure they provide service with a positive spirit and focus that is consistent with institutional philosophy.

- Conduct research on your students' attitudes about the roles their parents are playing in their collegiate experience. The Cooperative Institutional Research Program (CIRP) and National Survey of Student Engagement (NSSE) surveys, and several of the American College Testing (ACT) entering-student instruments have useful data about student and parent demographics and expectations. Attendance at college-sponsored events designed for parents is also a useful indicator of parent-institution expectations. Parent and family weekends on many campuses are increasingly elaborate in planning, price, and execution. Institutional researchers would be well-advised to monitor changes in student satisfaction relative to college-initiated efforts to include parents in the life of the institution.

- Review activities at other colleges and universities to determine which models of working with parents might be effectively adapted at your institution. Consistent with other programs and services in student affairs, parent programs at competitor and aspiration institutions should be monitored and benchmarked for comparison. Many professional conferences now routinely offer sessions on parent programs. Keep abreast of new developments in programming, expectations, and best practices for this emerging constituency.

- Be deliberate in the development of an institutional response to working with parents. In some cases, the development of a program with dedicated staff is appropriate. A more distributed institutional response may be better at other colleges and universities. In either scenario, an institution-wide advisory board should be developed to ensure thoughtful discussion of issues, and development and implementation of cost-effective programs and services.

References

Hoover, E. (2004, January 16). Parents united. *The Chronicle of Higher Education 50*(19), A35.

Immerwahr, J. (Spring 1998, #98-2). *The price of admission: The growing importance of higher education.* San Jose, CA: National Center for Public Policy and Higher Education.

Immerwahr, J. & Foleno, T. (May 2000, #00-2). *Great expectations: How the public and parents— White, African-American, and Hispanic—view higher education.* San Jose, CA: National Center for Public Policy and Higher Education.

Jaschik, S. (1990, August 15). Tuition probe ends its first year, colleges are confused. *The Chronicle of Higher Education 36*(48).

National Association of Student Personnel Administrators & American College Personnel Association. (January 2004). *Learning reconsidered: A campus-wide focus on the student experience.* Washington, DC: Authors.

Annotated Bibliography
Parent and Administrator Resources

Jeanette M. Barker and Kimberly G. Frazier

The purpose of this annotated listing of books, articles, and websites is to provide resources on parents and their involvement within higher education. This is not an exhaustive listing but one that provides college administrators and parents with resources beneficial in exploring the topic of parental involvement.

Books/Chapters

Austin. D. M. (1993). Orientation activities for the families of new students. In M.L. Upcraft, R.H. Mullendore, B.O. Barefoot, & D.S. Fidler (Eds.), *Designing successful transitions: A guide for orienting students to college.* (Monograph 13, 1st ed.) pp. 97-110. Columbia, SC: National Resource Center for The First-Year Experience and Students in Transition.

The focus of this chapter is on the ways in which orientation professionals can work with the important people in students' lives. The author addresses issues regarding parents; step-parents; guardians of traditional-age students; and the spouses/partners of nontraditional-age, adult learners. The author states that when working with students, it is of the utmost importance to understand the influence of the family system.

Barking, C. (1999). *When your kid goes to college; A parents survival guide.* New York: Avon Books Inc.

This book provides helpful information for parents, especially about networking with other parents whose children are going off to college. It offers advice on giving students the freedom to grow and develop, while still allowing them to balance their independence with parental dependence.

Barkley, N. (1993). *How to help your child land the right job: Without being a pain in the neck.* New York: Workman Publishing.

The author provides a step-by-step program to assist students in making career choices. She highlights how parents can assist their students in defining skills, interests, values, and goals. In addition, the author encourages parents to interact with their students through role-play in order to assist them in becoming more effective in interviews.

Bordy, J. (2000). *Bringing home the laundry: Effective parenting for college and beyond.* Dallas, TX: Taylor Trade Publishing.

Bringing Home the Laundry, by a clinical psychologist and family counselor, reveals the core issues facing parents and their college-bound children. These issues include dealing with separation anxiety, depression, decision making, and keeping in touch. The author identifies and explains parental behaviors that provide a secure foundation for children.

Coburn, K. L. & Treeger, M. L. (2003). *Letting Go: A parents' guide to understanding the college years* (4th ed.). New York: HarperCollins.

Letting Go leads parents through the period of transition that students experience between the junior year of high school and college graduation. The authors explain how to distinguish normal development stages from problems that may require parental or professional intervention. This new edition explains the differences between college life today and what parents may have experienced 20 or 30 years ago.

Cohen, R. (Ed.). (1985). *Working with the parents of college students: New Directions for Student Services, No. 32.* San Francisco: Jossey-Bass.

In this volume, invited authors explain and explore the following topics: (a) historical, legal, and psychological factors that led to institutions' noninvolvement with parents; (b) legislative base defining the Buckley Amendment of 1974; (c) college-parent relationships; (d) parents' involvement with the admissions process; (e) appropriateness and limitations of various parent orientation-program models; (f) assessment of parents' involvement in residence life matters; (g) how financial aid is balanced with the needs of parents; (h) family responses to student's academic failure and emotional difficulties; and (i) institutions' organization and delivery of services to parents.

Daniel, B. V. & Scott, B. R. (2001). *Consumers, adversaries, and partners: Working with the families of undergraduates. New Directions for Student Services, No. 94.* San Francisco: Jossey-Bass.

This book addresses how institutions can meet the changing needs of today's families of undergraduates. The authors review historical approach to family involvement and explore parents' roles today. The authors identify topics facing college administrators in their pursuit to partner with parents and increase student success.

Daniel-Tatum, B. (2003). *Why are all the black kids sitting together in the cafeteria? And other conversations about race (5ᵗʰ ed.).* New York: Basic Books.

The author addresses issues of diversity, race, and racism. She uses real-life examples to illustrate how conversations on racial identities are needed in enhancing communication across racial and ethnic groups.

DeBard, R. (2004). *Millennials coming to college: New Directions for Student Services, No. 106.* San Francisco: Jossey-Bass.

The chapters in this book provide an overview and understanding of the new generation of college students, the millennials. The authors critically examine the attitudes, beliefs, and behaviors of the millennial students and assert that student affairs practitioners will need to rethink student development theories and adopt new learning and service strategies in order to effectively educate and serve this generation of students. Other topics explore the historical and cultural influences that shape generations and the diversity in millennial students.

Harris, M. B. & Jones, S. L. (1996). *Helping your college student succeed: The parent's crash course in career planning.* Lincolnwood, IL: NTC Publishing Group.

This study identifies college student concerns and attempts to answer relevant career questions regardless of institution type or academic major. The authors, aware of the current career development processes and the volatile employment market, use their knowledge to offer parents suggestions and information that enable their student to feel competent and self confident, thus ultimately increasing their chances for career success.

Hatch, C. (2000). Parent and family orientation: Programs supporting student success. In M. J. Fabich (Ed.). *Orientation Planning Manual.* Pullman, WA: National Orientation Directors Association.

Parent orientation can meet both institution goals and national standards when audiences identify they have gained informed and useful knowledge of facts, circumstances, and situations they can expect their students to navigate during college. Educated on the implications of these factors, they can play a significant role in influencing student success by proactively supporting students through stages of academic, social, and emotional development.

Howe, N. (2003). *Millennials go to college: Strategies for a new generation on campus: Recruiting and admissions, campus life, and the classroom.* Washington, D.C.: American Association of Collegiate Registrars and Admissions Officers & LifeCourse Associates.

This book is designed for college administrators who are especially interested in adapting to a new population of collegians. The authors assert that today's incoming students are closer to their parents; focused on grades and performance; busy with extracurricular activities; eager to take part in community activities; savvy in technology; interested in mathematics and science; less interested in the humanities; demanding of a secure, regulated environment; and respectful of social conventions and institutions.

Howe, N. & Strauss, W. (2000). *Millennials rising: The next great generation.* New York: Vintage Books.

The authors conducted polls with hundreds of students, parents, and teachers. Their research findings help to explain the profile of a new generation of youth. Through the authors' research, they introduce a rising generation called the millennials. The authors accentuate that this new generation is smart, optimistic, and may bring a new revolution to America's campuses.

Johnson, H. E. & Schelhas-Miller, C. (2000). *Don't tell me what to do, just send money: The essential parenting guide to the college years.* New York: St. Martin's Griffin.

When children leave for college, many parents feel uncertain about their shifting roles. The authors emphasize the importance of parents being mentors to their college student, and assist parents on how to be an influential factor in the life of their student while still supporting

their independence. The authors offer insight into the minds of college students and provide parents with simple suggestions for improving communication with their children.

Lauer, J. & Lauer, R. (1999). *Survive and thrive in an empty nest: Reclaiming your life when your children have grown.* Oakland, CA: New Harbinger Inc.

"Empty Nest" is a rather bleak metaphor for a home in which the kids have "flown the coop," and for many parents, this can be a time of conflicting emotions ranging from feelings of grief and loss to relief and even exhilaration. But as the authors point out, it is also a time for new beginnings, a time to build upon old relationships, to expand personal interests and to set new direction for life.

Light, R. (2001). *Making the most of college: Students speak their minds.* Cambridge, MA: Harvard University Press.

The author uses the words of students to reveal their college experience in and out of the classroom. Over a 10-year period, he interviews 1600 Harvard seniors and shares their stories on how they learn, study, make choices, view their teachers, and deal with issues of diversity

MacKay, J. K. & Ingram, W. (2002). *Let the journey begin: A parent's monthly guide to the college experience.* Boston: Houghton Mifflin Company.

As parents and their first-year college student begin the school year, many questions may arise. Knowing what to ask will help parents maximize the benefits of attending transition programs such as parent orientations. This brief text includes innovative features and activities to help parents deal with the issues they and their first-year children face during the freshman year of college. It highlights the ongoing process of adjustment and is structured in eight sections to reflect the school-year cycle.

Mullendore, R. H. & Banahan, L. A. (2005). Designing orientation programs. In M. L. Upcraft, J. N. Gardner, & B. O. Barefoot (Eds.), *Challenging and supporting the first-year student: A handbook for improving the first year of college.* San Francisco: Jossey-Bass.

The authors provide rationale and structure for orientation programs for students and parents. The chapter addresses the differing needs of families of first-generation students, adult learners, commuting students, and community college students.

Mullendore, R. H. & Hatch, C. (2000). *Helping your first-year college student succeed: A guide for parents.* Columbia, SC: National Orientation Directors Association & National Resource Center for The First-Year Experience and Students in Transition.

This informational booklet focuses on "letting go" as a long-term process that should never be completed. The authors encourage parents to renegotiate their changing relationship with their student as an adult, and features 10 sections about the major events and feelings parents and students will likely experience during the first year of college. The authors offer suggestions for resolving these issues.

Newman, B. M. & Newman, P. (1992). *When kids go to college: A parents guide to changing relationships.* Columbus, OH: Ohio State University Press.

This guide will help answer important questions that parents have about their changing student as s/he enters college. The authors explain how to make the most of the exciting collegiate years. Topics covered in this book are: (a) identity formation, (b) values development, (c) career exploration, (d) social relationships, (e) sexuality, (f) alcohol and drug abuse, (h) romantic relationships, (i) residence hall life, (j) personal freedom, (k) depression, (l) discrimination, and (m) college bureaucracy.

Savage, M. (2003). *You're on your own: But I'm here if you need me: Mentoring your child during the college years.* New York: Fireside Books.

This book includes helpful information for parents. The author emphasizes important tips for college students as well as for parents. Incoming college undergraduates can demonstrate some irrational behavior that parents cannot always understand. This book explains issues from the parent's point of view as well as that of the student.

Upcraft, M. L., Gardner, J. N. and Associates (1989). *The freshman year experience: Helping students survive and succeed in college.* San Francisco: Jossey-Bass.

The Freshman Year Experience provides a blueprint for helping freshmen succeed, including specific and practical suggestions. The authors examine why freshmen succeed and the ways in which institutions can foster freshman success, focus on the value of freshman seminars, look at how institutions can be responsive to the diverse needs of freshmen, and stress the importance of building partnerships between faculty and student affairs professionals.

Van Steenhouse, A. (2002). *Empty nest . . . full heart: The journey from home to college.* Denver, CO: Simpler Life Press.

This book provides the support parents need when children leave for college. The author chronicles the tumultuous journey for students from the senior year of high school, through the challenging summer, to the first year of college. The author offers practical advice, through stories and passages, for handling each stage of the transition from high school to college.

Ward-Roof, J. A. & Hatch, C. (Eds.) (2003). *Designing successful transitions: A guide for orienting students to college,* (Monograph 13, 2nd edition).Columbia, SC: National Orientation Directors Association & National Resource Center for The First-Year Experience and Students in Transition.

The chapters in this monograph examine critical issues faced by orientation professionals, and provide organizational, theoretical, technological, and practical perspectives of college orientation programs.

Articles

Boyd, V. S, Hunt, P. F., Hunt, S. M., Magoon, T. M., & Van Brunt, J .E. (1997). Parents as referral agents for their first year college students: A retention intervention. *Journal of College Student Development, 38*(1), 83-84.

The researchers examined college retention by seeking to discover if the students of 150 parents, who were equipped with a resource directory of academic information, persisted at a higher level than the students whose parents did not receive the directory. Researchers found no significant differences among the comparison groups on rates of persistence, but found the students whose parents were part of the treatment group experienced better rates of persistence in good academic standing.

Feenstra, J. S., Banyard, V. L., Rines, E. N,. & Hopkins, K. R. (2001). First-year students' adaptation to college: The role of family variables and individual coping. *Journal of College Student Development, 42*(2), 106-113.

This study investigates the role of family structure, family conflict, family coping, and individual coping on adjustment to college. A total of 139 students (mean age 18.1; 78% women) were surveyed in their first semester of college. The research attempted to understand the importance of both family and individual coping in order to assist professionals who work with college students to understand why some students make more positive adjustments to college than others.

Forbes, K. J. (2001). Students and their parents: Where do campuses fit in? *About Campus, 6*(4), 11-17.

The author examines two central questions, what do students need from parents and what do students need from administrators and faculty? Analyses of the questions are explored through the changing role of the parent-student relationship. The author argues that parents today view in loco parentis to mean caretaking or nurturing, and that students' separation from parents actually occurs later in college. Therefore, the author suggests that administrators view themselves as facilitators in the student-parent separation process during this time of increased parental demands.

Gold, J. (1995). An intergenerational approach to student retention. *Journal of College Student Development, 36*(2), 182-187.

The effects of intergenerational family patterns on the student's adaptation to the college environment are presented. According to this approach, the college student moves from the family of origin to the university family, carrying family-sponsored messages about the university, success, separating from home, and individual identity. The author, through the use of two case studies, illustrates the application of student retention issues to preventive and remedial programs.

Hoover, E. (2004). Parents united. *The Chronicle of Higher Education, (50)*19, A35. Retrieved June 18, 2004 from http://chronicle.com/prm/ weekly/v50/i19/19a03501.htm

The author reviews the establishment and purpose of the College Parents of America. The author reports that the College Parents of America is a nonprofit group organized in 1998 to advocate for parents on higher education issues and address issues affecting campus life.

Janosik, S. M. (2001). Expectations of faculty, parents, and students for due process in campus disciplinary hearings. *Journal of College Student Development, 42*(2), 106-113.

The purpose of this research was to assess faculty, parent, and student expectations for due process protections in campus disciplinary hearings involving suspension and dismissal. Responding to a 20-item, researcher-developed questionnaire, a random sample of 464 faculty members, parents, and students indicated that they expect that high levels of due process will be provided in suspension-level campus disciplinary hearings; however, they differ on the importance of specific due process procedures.

Janosik, S. M. (2004). Parents' views on the Clery act and campus safety. *Journal of College Student Development, 45*(1), 43-56.

The author conducted a study to examine parents' knowledge of the Jeanne Clery Disclosure of Campus Security Policy and Campus Crime Statistics Act and their use of the information. A total of 435 parents participated in the study during summer orientation. The author found parents' knowledge and use to be low. Only 25% of the parents remembered reading the summary of the Clery Act they were provided before attending summer orientation. Additionally, the researcher found that responses to awareness strategies and college administrators who provided this information varied by educational attainment, experience with crime in the immediate family, and experience with children in college.

Johnson, H. E. (2004). Educating parents about college life. *The Chronicle of Higher Education, 50*(18), b11-12.

With the increase of parent involvement in the lives of college students, the author argues that universities and colleges do little to share their critical insight on the development of the college experience with parents. The author stresses that colleges and universities need to change how they relate to parents, and asserts that colleges and universities should use program opportunities (e.g., admission process, orientation) to help parents become effective partners in their student's development.

Lamadrid, L. (2002). Overfacilitation. *About Campus, 7*(1), 25-27.

The author defines overfaciltation as a way of doing for students what they should do for themselves. The author asserts that parents can avoid overfacilitation by acting in the role of a consultant, offering resources at their disposal and helping their student to problem solve. Further, the author argues that administrators and faculty can avoid overfacilation by creating a partnership with parents to facilitate the education of students.

Pearson, C. & Dellmann-Jenkins, M. (1997). Parental influence on a student's selection of a college major. *College Student Journal, 31,* 301-313.

The researchers examined the impact of parental educational background on the decision of incoming freshmen (n=655) to choose a college major. Researchers reported that parental educational background did not influence academic major decision. Further, the researchers noted group differences did exist related to parental encouragement influencing a student's decision to attend college, and that incoming college women were more decisive in choosing a major than men.

Taylor, J. & Taylor, S. (2004). Parents have their say . . . about their college-age children's career decisions. *NACAE Journal, 64*(2), 15-20.

Researchers surveyed parents' (n=493) beliefs relating to their incoming freshman student's career choice and the influences of those career choices. Researchers found that parents overwhelmingly ranked themselves as the most influential figures in their children's career development decisions. Only 38.5% of parents believed that they had very little influence on their children's career decisions, and 45.5% believed that they should have little to very little influence on career decisions.

Tierney, W. G. (2002). Parents and families in precollege preparation: The lack of connection between research and practice. *Educational Policy, 6*(4), 588-606.

The author critically examines the lack of connection between research and practice in the area of parent and family involvement in precollege preparation. The author asserts that there is an inconsistency between the research indication that parent and family involvement increases the chances of low-income students gaining entrance into college and the practice of family participation in college outreach programs.

Turrentine, C. G., Schnure, S. L., Ostroth, D. D., & Ward-Roof, J. A. (2000). The parent project: What parents want from the college experience. *NASPA Journal, 38*(1), 31-43.

The researchers developed an interactive website that invited parents to identify their top three hopes or goals for their students' first-year college experience. A total of 1382 parents participated in this 2-year qualitative study. Researchers report that quality education, job preparation, maturity/independence, fun/enjoyment, graduation, friendships/networks, and academic success were among the top-tier parental goals in this study.

Wintre, M. G. & Sugar, L. A. (2000). Relationships with parents, personality, and the university transition. *Journal of College Student Development, 41*(2), 202-213.

Relationships with parents and personality were examined as predictors of university adjustment among 419 first-year college students. The results provide some insight into practical implications that may ease the stress associated with the transition to college. The authors state that a practical implication is that the role of parents cannot be dismissed. Relationships based on mutual trust, open and honest communication, and equal treatment appear to be particularly beneficial in terms of facilitating adjustment.

Website Resources

http://www.collegeparents.org/

This is the College Parents of American website, which is dedicated to advocating and serving current and future college parents and students, and is the only national membership association for parents. The website provides a one-stop shop on critical resources relating to savings strategies, financial aid, scholarships, academic strategies, application and selection process information, and challenges and opportunities students and parents encounter during the college years.

http://www.edc.org/hec/parents/

This is the Higher Education Center: The Parent Connection website provides a comprehensive listing of resources for parents of college-bound students and addresses college drinking and drug use. A sampling of letters on what colleges and universities are saying about alcohol, drugs, and parental notification can be accessed on this website, along with information on several organizations and services for parents of college-age students.

National On-Campus Report [Internet version: http://www.magnapubs.com/student/index.html]

This newsletter reports on trends in campus life outside the classroom, and has addressed topics on families of undergraduate students, residence halls, marketing trends, counseling, student activities, campus security and other student affairs issues.

Parents, you're not done yet: [Internet version http://www.edc.org/hec/parents/centurycouncil.pdf]

This pamphlet, *Parents, you're not done yet,* is funded by America's leading distillers and created by the Century Council. The pamphlet provides helpful alcohol-related information and statistics for families of undergraduates. Free copies of the pamphlet are available from the Century Council.

University and College Websites for Parent & Family

Listed are selected university and college websites for parents and families, not an exhaustive listing. These websites provide comprehensive resource information for parent and family, and are easy to navigate.

Bowling Green State University
  http://www.bgsu.edu/offices/sa/parentfp/

Calvin College
  http://www.calvin.edu/parents/about_us.htm

Dartmouth College
  http://www.dartmouth.edu/~parents/

Dickinson College
  http://www.dickinson.edu/parents/

Syracuse University
  http://www.syr.edu/parfriends.html

University of Maryland
  http://www.terpparent.umd.edu/

University of Michigan
  http://www.umich.edu/parents/main/index.html

University of North Carolina Chapel Hill
  https://parents.unc.edu/

University of Southern California
  http://www.usc.edu/student-affairs/parent/

University of Wisconsin-Madison
  http://www.wisc.edu/wiscinfo/parents/

Higher Education Associations and Research Centers Websites

The following association websites may provide student affairs professionals and parents with additional reports, studies, policies, and procedures relating to families of undergraduates.

American Association of Collegiate Registrars and Admissions Officers (AACRAO)
  1 Dupont Circle N.W., Suite 330
  Washington, DC 20036
  (202) 293-9161
  www.aacrao.com

American College Health Association (ACHA)
  P.O. Box 28937
  Baltimore, MD 21240-8937
  (410) 859-1500
  http://www.acha.org

American College Personnel Association (ACPA)
  1 Dupont Circle N.W. Suite 300
  Washington, DC 20036
  (202) 835-2272
  http://www.acpa.nche.edu

American College Testing
  500 ACT Drive
  P.O. Box 168
  Iowa City, Iowa 52243-0168
  http://www.act.org

Association of College and University Housing Officers-International (ACUHO-I)
  941 Chatham Lane, Suite 318
  Columbus, OH 43221-2416
  (614) 292-0099
  http://www.acuho.ohio-state.edu/

College Board Headquarters
  45 Columbus Avenue
  New York, NY 1 0023-6992
  (212) 713-8000
  http://www.collegeboard.com

Cooperative Institutional Research Program (CIRP)
  3005 Moore Hall/Box 951521
  Los Angeles, CA 90095-1521
  (310) 825-1925
  http://www.gseis.ucla.edu/heri/freshman.html

National Association of Student Financial Aid
Administrators (NASFAA)
    1920 L Street N.W., Suite 200
    Washington, DC 20036
    (202) 785-0453
    http://www.nasfaa.org/

National Association of Student Personnel
Administrators (NASPA)
    1875 Connecticut Avenue N.W., Suite 418
    Washington, DC 20009
    (202) 265-7500
    http://www.naspa.org

National Orientation Directors Association (NODA)
    University of Michigan-Flint
    375 University Center
    Flint, Michigan 48502-1950
    (810) 424-5513
    http://www.nodaweb.org/

National Resource Center for The First-Year
Experience and Students in Transition.
    1728 College Street
    Columbia, SC 29208
    (803) 777-6229
    http://www.sc.edu/fye/

Appendix A
Model Programs

Beth Saul and Sarah Honor

American University in Dubai

Purpose

American University of Dubai (AUD) is a developing American-accredited university (Southern Association of Schools and Colleges, Washington, DC Licensure Commission) which was established in 1995. AUD is the one of the only American–accredited universities in the Arabian Gulf. The student population is 2000 and students represent over 70 nationalities. AUD has a developed Study Abroad program and welcomes American students every term. Students who graduate from AUD attend graduate and professional schools in the United States and Europe. The student services division has developed polices, procedures, and practices that mirror those of major American liberal arts universities. The division relies heavily on *Best Practices in Student Affairs,* a joint document by the American College Personnel Association (ACPA) and NASPA, and standards and guidelines for various areas of student services produced by the Council for the Advancement of Standards in Higher Education.

Program Description

AUD has a developed Parents' Orientation Program, now in its 5th year. Parents attend an afternoon session prior to the start of the semester. At this session, welcoming informative speeches are given by the dean of student services, the provost, and the president of the university. In addition, parents hear from AUD alumni, current students, and faculty. A question-and-answer session follows where parents are encouraged to voice their concerns and questions.

Parents also receive a *Parent Handbook* that overviews various aspects of the AUD experience. The AUD parent orientation is extremely important as students come from a wide variety of secondary school experiences. Acquainting parents with the objectives, goals, and characteristics of an American liberal arts

university experience is one of the most important goals of the program. Other topics include the purpose of parent orientation, parent's role in student's success, the transition between high school and university, AUD's mission & presence in the Gulf, the meaning of American education, academic expectations of AUD, and the freshmen year experience. Parents also receive information about how instructors conduct their classes, and the expectations and responsibilities of university students in an American system. Key identifiers of the American collegiate experience are one of the most important components of the program.

Program Assessment

Parents complete an evaluation immediately following the orientation. Parent orientation evaluations are distributed and collected by student orientation leaders. The evaluation focuses on five primary research questions:

1. How satisfied were parents with the overall orientation?

2. What did parents learn and plan to apply from the orientation?

3. What could be improved?

4. What activities should be eliminated?

The above research questions are heavily influenced by the work of Kirkpatrick (in Hanson, 1997) whose 4-stage evaluation framework is one of the norms in business evaluation theory and practice. Comprehensive program evaluations review participants' responses to training through their (a) reaction, (b) learning, (c) behavior, and (d) results.

A positive reaction indicates that participants are attentive and trying to absorb the information being presented. It also suggests that favorable information about the program is shared with colleagues and acquaintances. Glowing reactions do not ensure that learning has taken place; thus, in the Learning level, learning gains of participants are assessed. The behavior level is an appraisal of the participants' subsequent application of the learning. Lastly, the results level considers organizational as well as individual modifications and changes. This level documents the actual changes that occurred at large with an organization that can be directly linked to the training program (Hanson, 1997). Naturally, the more levels of the model that are considered, the more comprehensive the total evaluation is. Research questions in this evaluation are linked to the reaction and learning stages of the Kirkpatrick model of program evaluation. Any changes made to the orientation program are linked to the results stage of the model.

Hanson, J. B. (1997). *Common ground, Is it reachable? A program evaluation of a cross-cultural training program.* Unpublished doctoral dissertation, Purdue University, West Lafayette, IN.

Contact Information

Jennifer Hanson
Dean of Student Services
American University of Dubai
Tel: 971-4-399-9000
E-mail: jhanson@aud.edu

Bowling Green State University

Purpose

Bowling Green State University's (BGSU's) Parent and Family Programs' (PFP's) mission is to build a strong connection between parents and family members of BGSU students and the university. The program serves as a support and advisory body to parents, students, and the university by providing information that is beneficial to BGSU parents and family members, and by highlighting opportunities to become involved in university initiatives, activities, and events.

Program Description

Parent and Family Programs are designed to help parents and other family members of BGSU students. Our Falcon Family Advisory Board, an advisory council made up of parents, staff, faculty, and students, meets periodically throughout the year to plan the initiatives and activities of PFP. PFP also sponsors the Parents' Fund Drive through BGSU's office of development, an activity which helps to fund PFP's efforts. PFP also coordinates campus events, including Falcon Family Weekend, and participates in other campus events, including Move-In Weekend and Sibs 'n Kids, another campus-wide initiative to bring parents and family members to campus.

PFP also publishes *Parents' Connection,* a bi-yearly newsletter for the parents of undergraduate students. *Parents' Connection* highlights programs, initiatives, and issues of interest to BGSU students and families, and is an important informational resource. Lastly, in the fall of 2004, Parent and Family Programs inaugurated a topic-oriented e-newsletter series for Internet-connected parents.

Parent and Family Programs sponsors a website (http://www.bgsu.edu/offices/sa/parentfp/) containing valuable information about BGSU for parents and family members, including student and family transition issues, campus academic and involvement resources, and related issues of interest to parents and family members. PFP also operates a highly-utilized toll-free telephone helpline.

In addition, PFP offers an e-mail helpline (bgsupc@bgnet.bgsu.edu) for e-mail-equipped parents and family members who have questions. Parent and Family Programs also reaches out to family members in their home communities by hosting a series of regional meetings, held in the spring of each year in conjunction with the offices of alumni and admissions.

Program Assessment

Bowling Green State University PFP views program assessment as a cornerstone to success, and thus satisfaction-based surveys are created and administered to participants and guests at all major PFP programmatic efforts and special events. Further, regional meetings continue to be utilized as opportunities to gather parents and family members together in focus groups to yield richer data.

Contact Information

Cyndie Roberts
Bowling Green State University
Doctoral Intern
Office of Student Life
301 Bowen-Thompson Student Union
E-mail: crobert@bgnet.bgsu.edu
Tel: 419.372.2843
Fax: 419.372.0499

The College of Saint Rose

Purpose

The office of parent relations was established within the division of student affairs to facilitate, nurture, and enhance the relationship with the parents of the student community. The mission statement of the department states that "The office of parent relations is dedicated to providing consistent communication to parents and community members, while serving as a resource and as an advocate for parent issues and concerns on behalf of the educational mission of our students." The primary goals and objectives are: (a) to serve as a campus liaison between parents and departments or areas, (b) to assist parents in resolving concerns, and (c) to help the campus community understand how the office of parent relations may benefit individual departments.

The office of parent relations serves as the clearinghouse for most parent phone calls, e-mails, correspondence, and walk-ins that occur throughout the campus community. The director is primarily known as the campus "ombudsman."

Program Description

The parents of our first-year students meet the director during summer orientation. The director describes her role to parents as "serving as their 'best' friend." The parents are also introduced to the theme of the department: parents as partners. While the department values the importance of appropriate student development tasks being accomplished during a student's college journey, providing parents with resources on how to assist their student on this journey has been a priority. Parents have become

diplomatically trained on how to assist their student with problem-solving skills, decision-making skills, self-confidence in handling difficult situations, and overall competency within the college environment. Unlike many other campus programs, the office of parent relations does not solicit money for any fundraising programs. The primary program components include:

1. Coordination of a 2-day summer parent orientation program;

2. Development and distribution of a parent handbook;

3. Regular mailings to parents of first-year students regarding deadlines and important dates, opportunities for families to join in campus activities, and pertinent information regarding changes in policies and procedures;

4. Regular e-mail "blasts" and monitoring of a parent chat program;

5. Semester mailings to parents of upper-class students with information deemed useful for this cohort;

6. Representation of parent issues and concerns on campus-wide committees;

7. Primary source of communication in emergencies or crisis situations;

8. Primary source of communication in significant judicial cases.

Program Assessment

The program has a two-pronged assessment. Approximately 2 weeks following each phone call, e-mail, in-person contact, and/or regular mail contact, an anonymous evaluation is sent to the parent. Included is a preaddressed envelope to return the survey. This information is then summarized and evaluated for program effectiveness, timeliness of responses, and general satisfaction. For the more formal programs offered by the department, individual evaluation forms have been developed and distributed. Other more formal assessment measures are currently being researched and reviewed.

Contact Information

Wendy Neifeld Wheeler
Director of Parent Relations
The College of Saint Rose
432 Western Avenue
Albany, New York 12203
Tel: 518-458-5308
E-mail: wheelerw@strose.edu

Miami University

Purpose

From the opening sessions of new student orientation and registration to final conferral of diplomas at commencement, Miami University students enjoy a unique undergraduate educational experience offered in rural Oxford, Ohio. While miles and time zones may separate parents and families from students, Miami University takes steps to ensure that they become partners in the student experience. As the anchor of support for this contact, the parents office serves as a resource, providing a vital link to other offices and events on campus.

Program Description

In addition to parents' orientation and registration, the office of residence life and new student programs produces a colorful and comprehensive *Guide for Families* that is included in a packet of materials for parents. Helpful information is made available in one clear, concise guide for parents to peruse and use. While plenty of valuable knowledge is included, this guide also assists family members in understanding some of the issues most associated with the transitions in their relationships.

The efforts of the parents office take this relationship further, providing a vital communication gateway for parents and family members to the rest of the campus community. *Weemakiki,* published tri-annually, serves as the official newsletter for Miami University parents and family members welcoming them into an ongoing relationship with the university and those that serve the students they love. Coming from the Miami Indian tribal language, the word "weemakiki" translates as

"my relatives." The office also maintains a website providing specific links to key information, as well as an archive of parent newsletters and other important announcements. The parents office assists in Parents Weekend and Kidsfest, two annual weekends designed to bring a touch of home back to campus for Miami students. Parents Weekend, held typically in October, provides all relatives the opportunity to come and share in the Miami experience, with informational sessions regarding Miami academic programs, cultural opportunities on campus and in the city of Oxford, and plenty of opportunities to share a good meal! Kidsfest, held typically in late spring, invites younger siblings—future Redhawks aged 14 and under—to campus for age-appropriate entertainment and the opportunity to experience collegiate life with their older Miami siblings.

Parents and family members also receive outreach from the Miami University Council, an organization that exists to encourage mutual understanding and to facilitate communication between parents and the university. Comprised of a group of dedicated parents, the council represents parents of various geographical areas and all undergraduate students. Members initiate special programs, support students through the Parents Fund, recruit new parent members, develop effective communication strategies for important parent information, and serve as leaders in building the Miami University Parents Fund.

The Parents Fund is a gift program led by Miami's director of development for student affairs, and enhances the experience for Miami students in several ways: (a) to recognize student leadership and service contributions to the campus and community, (b) to facilitate faculty/student interaction, (c) to provide opportunities for students to obtain career and service leadership experience, and (d) to promote students helping students through peer-delivered programming.

While such a list of activities and initiatives may be common at other universities, Miami once again seeks to strive further in reaching parents in today's world of instant communication. All parents and family members of first-year students are invited to receive *The Parent Lantern,* a new electronic newsletter sent via e-mail to give an update on the latest news and information parents can use to remain connected to the Miami community.

Program Assessment

Programming for Miami parents and families is a direct result of accurate assessment and ongoing evaluation practices. Parents have multiple opportunities for feedback, beginning with an online electronic evaluation at the end of summer orientation sessions. In addition, each issue of *Weemakiki* includes an area for parents to respond and send in or e-mail questions, and an "Ask Miami" service is available in *The Parent Lantern* that allows parents to submit a question, voice a concern, or provide feedback on any topic.

In an era of increased connections despite wide distances, Miami University shows exemplary service in reaching out to parents to build a strong partnership in educating the next generation of future Miami graduates.

Contact Information

Dan Schniedermeier
Parents Office Intern
Miami University
Oxford, Ohio
E-mail: schniedj@muohio.edu

Mt. San Antonio College

Purpose

The counseling department at Mt. San Antonio College (MTSAC), the largest single-district community college in California, tried in 1998 a new approach to increase student's success in college—orientation sessions for the new student's parents. As counselors we had seen a steady increase in inquiries from parents as to "What is the best major for my child?" "How many students transfer to the University?" "What services are available to my child?" To answer these questions and many more, the parent orientation program was developed.

The program introduces the parents to the climate of MTSAC and the expectations of what lies ahead for

their student. It also provides a vehicle for parents to connect and form important partnerships with their students and MTSAC. Family members are viewed as an important support system for students.

The primary objectives are to: (a) teach parents how to be a support for their students' success, (b) obtain information regarding parents who would be mentors and potential employers to MTSAC students, and (c) market MTSAC programs and services for re-entry parents—potential new students.

Program Description

Four 2-hour workshops are held prior to the start of the semester. Each parent is given a handbook. Those parents that have other children in college share their experiences with the other parents. Most of the sessions are held after 5:30 p.m., with some offered on Saturdays. For those parents that don't speak English, we also offer two extra sessions in Spanish with a Spanish translation of the parent handbook.

The areas covered by the orientation are as follows:

1. Overview of career counseling and a discussion about the process of choosing a major.

2. Presentation of all student services.

3. Discussion on time-management—balancing work and school and how it affects the family.

4. Explanation of how to transfer to the university.

5. Predictable crises that parents can anticipate; the decreasing control that parents can expect over their child's lives and the boundary issues as to what college staff can share with parents.

6. Identified costs and financial aid available.

Program Assessment

At each workshop, parents fill out an evaluation form. When they are returned there is a drawing and one parent wins a MTSAC mug. It guarantees that all the evaluation forms are returned. At the bottom of the evaluation form we request parents to fill in their name, telephone number, e-mail address and occupation, if they are interested in being contacted by MTSAC students, have employment opportunities, or would be interested in serving on an advisory board for a specific department. A resource guide is then assembled with this information that is disseminated to department chairs, counselors, and students. The feasibility and overall success of the parent orientations is based on the number of parents that attend and the satisfaction of these parents with the orientations. So many colleges throughout the U.S. have chosen to devote resources to the orientation of family members, but very few community colleges have chosen to do the same. As a result we have become a model for other community colleges in California.

Contact Information

Helen Lawrence
Counselor/Professor
Mt. San Antonio College
Tel: 909-594-5611 ext. 5925
E-mail: hlawrenc@mtsac.edu

San Diego State University

Purpose

San Diego State University (SDSU) believes that parental involvement contributes to student success. Begun in 1981 as a part-time program, the Aztec Parents Program is housed in the division of student affairs in the office of new student and parent programs and is staffed by a full-time director, a coordinator of parent programs, a coordinator of new student programs, one full-time support staff and two student interns.

Our Aztec Parents Program is designed around four key functions: (a) parent education, (b) parent communications, (c) parent involvement, and (d) parent fundraising. These four functions serve many purposes, including (a) developing a strong Aztec parents program identity on campus; (b) educating the parents advisory board about important university issues; (c) establishing campus-wide relationships by inviting parents to special functions; (d) surveying parents; (e) involving parents in strategic planning; (f) also involving parents in award selections and

committee work; and (g) developing Aztec parent leadership giving to the Parents Annual Fund.

During parent orientation and new student and family convocation, parents of new students are educated about SDSU's student programs and services. At orientation, parents of first-year and transfer students receive a handbook, a campus resource card with office names and numbers, and the parents' hotline number (a direct number to our parent programs coordinator). Parents also receive, throughout their student's enrollment, a quarterly newsletter, access to the campus library and career services, discounted logo items at the campus bookstore, and invitations to Family Weekend and various regional meetings. Family Weekend is purposely scheduled 6 to 8 weeks into the fall semester to coincide with the critical transition period that new freshmen and their family experience. It provides parents and students the opportunity to reconnect and to view the university as a new home away from home. Family Weekend, regional meetings, the parent newsletter, and our parents' hotline all help to keep Aztec parents connected to their students' college experience.

Program Description

One stellar aspect of the Aztec Parents Program is our Aztec parents advisory board. The role of this board is to advise the vice president for student affairs on student life issues at SDSU. The board consists of 25 parent volunteers who meet three times each academic year to discuss issues, such as student wellness, alcohol and other drug prevention/intervention, student retention, how technology supports student learning, dining services and public safety. They then give their feedback to student affairs' administrators.

One very special way that the vice president for student affairs involves the Aztec parents advisory board is by soliciting their recommendations on Aztec parent grant proposal requests from campus administrators, faculty, and staff each fall. Board members review the grant proposals prior to their first fall semester board meeting. At the meeting, they collectively rank the proposals and make recommendations on the level of funding for each one. Subsequently, the assistant vice president for student affairs meets with the vice president about the board's recommendations, and the vice president decides the final ranking and level of funding for each proposal.

The goal of the Aztec Parents Fund is to enhance or create programs and services that directly benefit the majority of students at San Diego State University.

Program Assessment

Outcomes of the SDSU Aztec Parents Program are: (a) better informed parents, (b) a smooth transition to the university experience for both students and parents, (c) parent connection to the Aztec family, (d) open channels of communication between parents and the university, and (e) additional personal and financial support to the university and its student programs.

Specific parent programs such as Parent Orientation and Family Weekend are assessed yearly through an online evaluation system. Parents provide feedback that allows us to adjust and enhance our programs to meet their needs. In addition, parents maintain contact with the coordinator of parent programs via the parents' hotline—a direct line to a real person when they need it. The calls are logged and assessed as to needs and trends. In this way, our Aztec Parents Program continues to grow and evolve, keeping abreast of the current needs of parents and students.

Contact Information

Eric Rivera
Assistant Vice President for Student Affairs
    Administration
Division of Student Affairs
San Diego State University
5500 Campanile Drive
San Diego, CA 92182-7430
Tel: 619.594.5211
Fax: 619.594.7089
E-mail: erivera@mail.sdsu.edu

Texas Tech University

Purpose

Parent Relations provides programs, services, and activities designed to enhance student learning and the support and retention of students by meeting the educational, informational, and involvement needs of their parents and families. Also home to the Texas Tech Association of Parents (better known as Tech Parents), Parent Relations serves all parents, families, and students, and works in partnership with the association to accomplish both groups' missions.

Tech Parents' mission is to serve as a unified voice for parents, to forge strong bonds and build bridges of mutual support between parents, their students and Texas Tech, and to foster parent participation and involvement. An all-volunteer, incorporated nonprofit organization, it is financed entirely by contributions and memberships. Tech Parents will celebrate its 50th Anniversary in 2006.

Parent relations is a university department within the division of student affairs, funded in part by student service fees. In a unique working partnership, Tech Parents serves as the involvement arm of the Parent Relations mission. The partnership facilitates its membership, leadership, and endowment growth, all of which are strategic goals. Tech Parents funds or assists in funding mutually beneficial programs and publications, in addition to other worthy programs. Parent Relations provides staff support for Tech Parents.

Program Description

Probably our most unique program to date is the "Road Raiders" Safe Travel Parent Network. Approximately 2,500 Tech Parents members from across the state and nation have volunteered to assist Tech students and parents as they travel away from home, whether it be an emergency, needed road break, or information. The entire list is printed in order of city/town in the university daily student newspaper prior to each holiday break or travel period. It is available for viewing or download on the website. Printed lists are distributed at new student orientation and at student functions. The list is also included in the parent handbook.

This network resulted from a parent suggestion at a Tech Parents membership meeting, and has had a phenomenal impact on both students and parents. The student body voted the Tech Parents as the "best student service" that year. Parents feel safer about their students driving long, desolate Texas distances, can do something of importance from their hometown, and provide a great service to the university. Road Raiders themselves never tell us how much they do—we hear the great stories from students and parents who called on them through the annual program survey. Assessments reflect high degrees of parent volunteer participation/retention and of student and parent familiarity with and confidence in using this resource.

Other Parent Relations programs and services include: (a) Developing and presenting or facilitating transitions programs for parents at new student orientation and educational/informational parent programs throughout the year; (b) distributing information through the parent website at http://www.parent.ttu.edu, toll free parent hotline, responses to parent@ttu.edu, and both electronic and printed parent publications; (c) gathering and maintaining parent information/emergency contact information, including the parent e-mail distribution system; (d) coordinating and distributing parent profile research; and (e) providing parent advising/coaching, problem solving, and referral.

Publications include *The Parent's Guide* handbook, *The Extension Cord* parent magazine, monthly *Parent e-News* and periodic e-lerts via e-mail, *Especially for Parents* brochure for newly admitted students' parents, Family Weekend mailer, and parent orientation checklist.

Other Tech Parents partnership endeavors include:

- 56 student scholarships awarded annually through the scholarship endowment, and 21 new one-time scholarship awards added during summer orientation

- distinguished visiting professorship endowment bringing Nobel Laureate annually

- 12 annual "Student Academic-Citizenship Awards"

- four annual faculty awards for excellence in teaching, research, and leadership

- Family Weekend in the fall and Scholarship Weekend in the spring

- Aloha Parents move-in event

- Junior Raiders for siblings 12 and under

- Leadership Express leadership development program for parents

- parent awards and volunteer recognitions

- area/chapter student send-offs and activities, such as finals goodie bags, holiday charter buses home, charters to Family Weekend

- partnership funding for student-led programs such as the Drowsy Driving Campaign, Finals Stress Breaks, Neighbor-To-Neighbor, etc.

Program Assessment

Both Parent Relations and Tech Parents operate under published strategic plans, which are updated and assessed annually through Texas Tech University's integrated institutional processes. Both qualitative and quantitative measures are included.

Contact Information

Trudy S. Putteet, Director
Parent Relations Office
Texas Tech University
244 West Hall
Box 42024 TTU
Lubbock, Texas 79409-2024
Tel: 806-742-3630
Toll free: 1-888-888-7409
Fax: 806-742-0330
E-mail: trudy.putteet@ttu.edu or parent@ttu.edu
Website: http://www.parent.ttu.edu

University of California Riverside

Purpose

To inform and support the parents of University of California Riverside (UCR) housing residents, initially upon enrollment and continually throughout the year.

Program Description

During orientation we have a parent track that includes sessions on how to support your student, FERPA guidelines, housing information, campus safety, and resources that are available. During the 2-day orientation session, the parents are offered the opportunity to stay in a residence hall room and eat in the dining facilities.

On move-in day, housing/dining services serves all of our areas with continental breakfast, fruits, cookies, and beverages throughout the day. Housing hosts several parent welcomes in each of our facilities on move-in day that allow the parents to meet the resident directors of that specific building, the assistant director, the associate director, the director of housing services, and representatives from the Parent Association and the alumni center. At each of these sessions the parents receive a parent handbook (also available online) and a goodie bag that includes:

- an "I am a proud parent of a UCR student" pen,

- a photo magnet that says, "Proud UCR Parent,"

- a magnet where parents can write the name and phone number of their student's resident director,

- a UCR parent license plate holder,

- a bookmark with suggestions on how to support their student, and

- a packet of Kleenex with a note from the Director that includes his e-mail address.

Parents are encouraged to e-mail any of us if they have a question or a concern.

The Parent Association meets quarterly in the residence halls allowing them the ability to have a support group, see what is happening on campus, receive a housing newsletter, and visit with students. The director of housing services attends these meetings to answer any parent concerns and to give updates on what is new at UCR Housing.

The Student Association and the Resident Hall Association give the parents several opportunities to send finals relaxers or motivational items to students during the school year. In addition dining services offers the opportunity to order birthday cakes and have them delivered to the students.

Program Assessment

Parents are asked to complete a survey of how UCR housing services is doing. The survey is included in the quarterly parent newsletter and mailed, postage paid, back to housing services. Results are then tallied and compared from year-to-year to assist us in evaluating and improving our program.

Contact Information

Jeanette Bradeen
Assistant Director of Housing, Residence Life
Housing Services
University of California Riverside
Tel: 951-827-6500
E-mail: jeanette.bradeen@ucr.edu

University of Central Florida

Purpose

Orientation services at the University of Central Florida (UCF) has developed successful programs and methods of assisting today's college families. From specialized websites to orientation programs, UCF disseminates important information and offers constant support to parents and families as they matriculate and transition with their college students. Parents, like students, want to be informed, encouraged, connected with each other, and given the tools for a successful future.

Program Description

Most recently, a section of the department's website (http://orientation.ucf.edu/parents/) has been dedicated to parents and family members of new students in an effort to ease the transition process into UCF. Three main subsections of the Parent & Family Information website are designed as "lists of things to do." By outlining and explicating the plethora of tasks requiring completion "Before attending orientation,"

"During orientation," and "After orientation," the lengthy process is made less daunting and increasingly manageable. This website also includes resources such as the following: (a) Frequently asked questions, (b) access to all presentations shared at orientation; (c) a calendar of campus events, (d) important academic dates, (e) timelines when new students face typical issues, (f) management strategies for these issues; and finally, (g) local accommodations for trips to UCF.

Nearly 6,000 parents and family members attend UCF orientation. Parents and family members of incoming first-year students are afforded the opportunity to have their own orientation program. Their program— 2 days concurrent but separate from their students' program—is found to be unique. Information given to students and parents is essentially the same but presented in format and sequence most appropriate for the respective populations. Some highlights of the parents' program include: (a) college meetings with academic deans, (b) a session on academic expectations, (c) presentations by various on-campus services and offices, and "Letting Go." Because the parent-student relationship undergoes metamorphosis during the college years, Letting Go offers successful strategies in helping parents reconnect with their students during this time of developmental change. Parents also meet with an orientation team leader, specifically trained to accompany and assist family members during orientation. Through questions and discussions, parents learn more about UCF through the eyes and experiences of a current UCF student. Finally, while at a family ice cream social, parents and family members play people bingo, learn about UCF's Alumni and Parent Association, win prizes, and most importantly, meet and talk with other parents whose students are also transitioning into UCF. Parents and families who build relationships and networks amongst each other create potential resources for their UCF experience.

Parents and families receive many resources while attending the 2-day program. They receive a calendar similar to that on the orientation services website. A handbook containing policies and procedures, information on services and offices both on and off campus, as well as academic majors can be located in their materials. A *FUTURE* newspaper, a parent guide by the National Orientation Directors Association,

and handouts from all the presentations round out the parent "bag o'goodies."

In addition to the program for first-year families, orientation services facilitates a one-day program for parents and family members of transfer students. This program, although shorter than the 2-day program, is very similar in format, content, and purpose. Participants hear from various university representatives who share information on typical issues and challenges transfer students face, as well as available services to students. Addressing issues from transfer credit to relocating to a larger campus is the "Transfer Student Success" presentation. Other elements shaping the family orientation are lunch with their students, a family reception, and a session with current students (the O-Team.) As the first-year families receive a "bag o' goodies," so, too, do the transfer parents and families receive the same resources.

Program Assessment

Evaluation and assessment have contributed to successful orientation programs and resource development. Participants of both first-year and transfer family orientations receive evaluation forms in their handbooks, to be completed and returned before departure. Questions refer to all medium of services rendered—usefulness of the website, comprehensiveness of the programs, and accessibility to resources. Results are calculated from each orientation, compiled and sent to university representatives who benefit from receiving said feedback, and inputted into the department's institutional effectiveness plan. Only through evaluation and assessment can UCF provide better assistance for future Golden Knights and their families.

Contact Information

Joe Ritchie, Director
Orientation Services
E-mail: jritchie@mail.ucf.edu
and
Eric Hennes, Assistant
E-mail:ehennes@mail.ucf.edu
University of Central Florida

Howard Philips Hall, Suite 218
Orlando, FL 32816-3240
Website: http://www.orientation.ucf.edu
Tel: 407.823.5105
Fax: 407.823.3847

University of Missouri–Columbia

Purpose

To work with the parents of University of Missouri–Columbia (MU) students, as partners, to create programming for parents that helps them help their students succeed. Through a variety of initiatives, MU focuses on introducing parents to the developmental and experiential issues their students will face as a college student; identifying the resources available to both students and parents; helping parents stay up-to-date on events and issues at MU; and identifying and developing resources that will benefit the educational experiences of students.

Program Description

The University of Missouri–Columbia utilizes a multifaceted approach to parent programming with an emphasis on front loading while providing on-going informational updates on services, resources, and events. These efforts include:

• A specialized track at orientation programs for new students prior to the start of each semester. At these programs parents are introduced to issues surrounding FERPA, campus safety, billing procedures, community living, faculty expectations, and the multitude of resources available to students and parents. Parents get to meet a high-level administrator (chancellor, provost, etc.) during their visit, indicative of the university's interest in their concerns and hopes.

• A parents' handbook providing a list of campus resources, descriptions, and contact information available at either orientation or during campus visits.

• Separate "opt-in" newsletters produced by residential life and the MU Parents Association (MUPA) providing on-going updates.

• Special parent-only information sessions during new student move-in emphasizing the shifting roles in the parent-student relationship, and encouraging parents to adopt a "coaching" mentality to help their students develop independence and important life skills. Parents are encouraged NOT to return to campus until Family Weekend, nearly a month later.

• Partnering with MUPA to identify parent concerns through direct contact with members of the board of directors and their constituents, as well as opportunities for supporting the university's educational mission either through fiscal contribution or direct involvement (e.g., a past president of the board currently sits on the advisory council of our Student Success Center).

Past fiscal support has led to the building of a new black culture center, improved lighting of a student union, funding for two graduate assistants for parent programming efforts, and creation of a campus landmark promoting our institutional values. In Columbia, St. Louis, and Kansas City, the board also hosts regional meetings for their more than 2,000 dues-paying members which include town hall meetings with high-level university administrators.

The MUPA is midway through a restructuring in their recruitment program that has taken them from a 400 member organization to an anticipated 4,000 plus members by the fall of 2006.

Program Assessment

Assessment of parent programmatic efforts is achieved through a variety of methods including a customer service and needs-assessment survey at summer orientation, feedback from the monthly MUPA board of directors meeting, MUPA surveys, and e-mails and phone calls to the department of student life.

Contact Information

David Rielley
Coordinator, New Student Programs
Tel: (573) 882-3621
E-mail: RielleyD@missouri.edu

University of North Carolina at Chapel Hill

Purpose

The Parents Council at the University of North Carolina at Chapel Hill as evolved significantly over the past 2 decades. The following description will demonstrate how careful attention to the history, mission, and expansion of this group has resulted in worthwhile outcomes and strong partnerships. It comes as no surprise that as parental involvement increases in the lives of college students, a greater interest in being involved in a parents' council program mirrors that movement. Just as parents are asked to partner in new ways with their students, institutions of higher education must partner in new ways with parent councils.

Chartered in 1789, the University of North Carolina at Chapel Hill has a long history of student self-governance, tradition, and alumni pride. Two centuries later, to support a growing parental involvement, a Parents Council was formed to serve as the leadership arm of the Carolina Parents Association. Initially, the council's purpose was to facilitate communication between parents and promote the development of the university by supporting the Carolina Parents Fund. Today, the council's purpose has expanded to include sponsoring programs and services that meet the needs of parents and involving parents in the life of the University community.

Program Description

Established in 1985 with 40 members, the Parents Council has grown rapidly to 185 members in 2004. Originally housed in the university's development office, the council's primary focus was fundraising. Over time, the council was transitioned to student affairs, while maintaining a strong partnership with the development office. By 1997, the Parents Council significantly changed its focus with increased attention to outreach, active participation in the university community, and advocacy for enhancements of student life. Embedded in the council's approach is a philosophy of being involved, accessible, responsive, and proactive in the support of student life and learning.

Today, the Parents Council includes an executive committee, consisting of national chairs, past national chairs, emeritus chairs, class chairs for each of the undergraduate classes, committee chairs to address areas of identified need, and at-large members. The vice chancellor for student affairs, or his/her designee, and the coordinator of parent programs serve as ex officio members. Each year, the full council meets twice and the executive committee meets six to eight times. Council members working in collaboration with the Carolina parents office host admitted-student receptions, summer send-offs, parent-orientation sessions, and the Carolina Parents Association meeting and its activities during the annual fall family weekend. Each year, the Parents Council grants monies for programs and services that support student life and learning both in and outside the classroom. Members of the council also serve on university committees to address areas such as academic advising and fraternity/sorority life.

Program Assessment

The Parents Council program at the University of North Carolina at Chapel Hill is assessed by a variety of methods to measure fundraising success, granting capabilities, program satisfaction, parent learning outcomes, and overall program achievement as compared to peer institutions. These methods involve tracking financial figures, compiling attendance records, distributing surveys regarding parent satisfaction and learning, identifying successful partnerships, and examining best practices at other institutions across the country. In addition, the Parents Council recently conducted a self-study for the purpose of long-range planning.

Assessment results indicate that the University of North Carolina at Chapel Hill has a strong Parent Council program. Particular highlights include: (a) self-supporting Parents Council; (b) parent-funded parents office, (c) a Parents Association open to all parents without charge, (d) numerous grant requests for innovative programs and services, and (e) strong partnerships with the development office, alumni affairs, college of arts & sciences, student government, and several departments within student affairs.

With success comes challenge. Particular challenges with recent growth of the Parents Council include impact on the parents office staff's workload, increased number of ethical dilemmas posed by parents, ability to stay focused, and financial implications for hosting meetings. Despite these challenges, parental involvement through a large Parents' Council is of value to the institution in that it benefits the bottom line: students' education through improved services and programs.

Contact Information

Sheila Hrdlicka, Coordinator of Parent Programs
University of North Carolina at Chapel Hill
CB#5105, Nash Hall
Chapel Hill, North Carolina 27599-5105
Tel: (919) 962-8304
Fax: (919) 962-4725
E-mail: Hrdlicka@email.unc.edu or parents@unc.edu
Website: http://parents.unc.edu

University of North Carolina at Greensboro

Purpose

College parents want to be involved in their children's lives. Partnering with parents is proving successful at the University of North Carolina at Greensboro (UNCG). In partnering, we have respect for the parents' role in the lives of their children and our students.

The UNCG Parent and Family program is a comprehensive collection of services designed to meet the needs of families. With staff dedicated to the program, we make it a priority to listen and respond with the parent perspective in mind. From a simple display of helpful items especially for parents in our bookstore, to our annual Family Weekend, we are engaged partners in the college experience. And we are committed to the idea that while these are our students, they are indeed, their children.

Program Description

It's about respect.
Rather than isolating parents with FERPA or a "Letting Go" presentation, we invite them into our community.

Parent and Family Orientation is designed to give more than the necessary information about campus resources. We give parents our respect by giving them attention and support. We give attention through opportunities to learn and ask questions. Support is cheerfully delivered though quality programs.

It's about empathy.
During student orientation leader training, we talk about the purpose of parent and family orientation and how to be empathetic to parents' concerns. How do we do that? Orientation leaders take on the role of parents in simulations of parent activities, such as "Expect the Unexpected," an interactive issues-based program. We include our leaders' parents in training by asking them to express in writing how it feels to send a child to college. We then share their responses with the leaders and process resultant emotions. We teach that parent concerns are to be addressed with respect. We stress that the parent and student programs are equal in importance. In the end, parents tell us that the level of care and maturity demonstrated by our orientation leaders is meaningful and moving.

It's about connection.
Family Weekend is our annual celebration, reuniting students with family members. Families get a second look at our campus and attend activities which bring students, parents, siblings, and friends together, building lasting memories.

Parents stay connected by joining the Parent Family Association and get involved by serving on the Parent-Family Advisory Council. Council members meet twice annually to discuss issues and learn about our community. Members' ideas are shared with the university community with the intention of having their collective voice heard and influencing change. Council members are also involved in our orientation and Family Weekend programs, welcoming parents into our community.

It's about communication.
We strive to keep communication lines open beyond orientation. Parents who join our Parent Family Association receive a monthly e-newsletter, *Family Connections*. Each month, we update families on events at UNCG and around Greensboro; post articles by

students, parents, and UNCG staff members, and links to resources online. Twice a year, parents receive our newsletter, *Family Matters,* which contains articles about current issues and events, as well as a Q-&-A section devoted to answering questions from parents. We communicate with families regularly by providing a useful website containing information on events and links to resources beneficial to parents of college students. Additionally, we offer a LISTSERV for sharing urgent information, such as hazardous weather conditions.

Program Assessment

It's about accountability.

In order to provide programs and services that truly matter and make a difference in the lives of students' families, we need to know what families want and need from us. Each program we offer for families is regularly assessed by using surveys and focus group interviews. After we analyze the data, we use it. We provide the feedback to various campus committees and program facilitators so they may make appropriate adjustments. During program planning, the results are reviewed and used in our decision making. The Parent Family Advisory Council serves as a sounding board for us as well. During our spring meeting, we discuss the assessment results and ask the council to help us meet the needs of families through their suggestions.

It's about partnering.

Partnering is working with others toward a common goal. At UNCG, partnering with parents is integral to the success of our Parent and Family Programs and ultimately, the success of our students, their children.

Contact Information

Kim Sousa-Peoples
Director of Orientation
E-mail: ksp@uncg.edu
and
Lindsey Pugh
Graduate Assistant, Orientation
E-mail: lkpugh@uncg.edu
University of North Carolina at Greensboro
Tel: 336-334-5231
Fax: 336-334-3823
Website: http://ori.dept.uncg.edu

University of Southern California

Purpose

The office for parent programs serves as a communication vehicle and resource center for Trojan parents. The office supervises and assists the University of Southern California (USC) Parents' Council and the USC Parents' Association and has the primary responsibility for the planning of Trojan Parents' Weekend. The office has no development responsibilities, but cooperates with the development office for the benefit of the Parents' Annual Fund and other donations.

Program Description

To foster a strong presence of communication, an elaborate website was developed with an interactive question feature which is answered on a daily basis. A semiannual newsletter and advice brochures from the parent and student perspective provide the main sources of on-going communication.

During new student orientation, the office for parent programs hosts a coffee on the first day with participation from the USC Parents' Council as greeters. The office for parent programs presents a Microsoft® PowerPoint® presentation on the 2nd day which describes all of the resources and programs for Trojan parents to all incoming freshmen parents. The office also staffs a table at the student affairs expo, attends the parent luncheon, and circulates at the closing parent reception.

The largest project for the office for parent programs is the planning of Trojan Parents' Weekend, a 4-day fall event. This event showcases USC's distinguished faculty, performance and athletic events, and college parenting and involvement workshops. In addition, resident faculty host events for their students and parents. Several meal events also are planned including an opening dessert reception, breakfast and lunch on Friday, and a tailgate picnic on Saturday 3 hours before kickoff.

The Office for Parent Programs has created a Parent Coordinating Council composed of representatives from all offices and schools that also have programs for parents. This council includes the ethnic offices, development, various schools with specific parent programs, orientation, and the USC Parents' Council officers. Through meetings every 6 to 8 weeks, everyone stays informed on a broader basis.

All Trojan parents are members of the USC Parents' Association. The Parents' Council is the leadership arm of the USC Parents' Association. Nine new families are added to the Parents' Council each fall through an application process to ensure diversity and representation throughout the university. Copresidents serve for a term of 2 years. The Parents' Council is organized into several committees including: outreach, events, recognition, fundraising, and teaching and mentoring awards (a project in cooperation with the provost's office). The council sponsors an annual dinner/basketball event in the spring. Its fundraising includes several Trojan spirit items which help to defray the cost of the teaching and mentoring awards and other Parents' Council events.

All Trojan parents are encouraged to participate in the parent testimonial program which provides authentic feedback on the university parent experience to both the office of admissions and the office for parent programs. In addition, all Trojan parents are encouraged to honor faculty who have made a positive difference for their students by submitting a parent nomination for the USC Parents' Association teaching and mentoring awards. In addition to the parent nomination, a supplementary student nomination and curriculum vitae from the faculty provide the provost's office with a more complete picture of the faculty's contribution in their review of nominee applications. The parents' committee mentioned above makes the final selections after the provost's review. These awards are presented during Trojan Parents' Weekend following the presidential address and include a $1,000 honorarium.

Program Assessment

The office for parent programs utilizes various methods of assessment. After Trojan Parents' Weekend, an online evaluation form is sent to each family that registers. A log is kept of parent phone calls to determine trends

and needs, and the USC Web-visitor question feature provides continuous information about parent concerns. Focus groups are also used as a source of feedback on current and future programs. The Parent Coordinating Council and the USC Parents' Council are a regular source of assessment through meeting discussions. Feedback from senior administration has been valuable in setting the institution's vision and direction for the office for parent programs in its first 2 years.

Overall, the office for parent programs provides a home for Trojan parents to serve this constituency as partners in their students' academic success.

Contact Information

Beth Saul, Director
Office for Parent Programs
University of Southern California
Student Union 200
Los Angeles, CA 90089-4892
Tel: 213-740-2080
Fax: 213-749-9781
E-mail: saul@usc.edu
Website: http://www.usc.edu/parent

Collegiate Parents

Website: http://www.collegiateparents.com

This is the website of Collegiate Parents which develops customized programs for parents of college-bound students to address their needs throughout the process of transitioning to a new parenting role with their child. Collegiate Parents conducts workshops for parents in high schools and colleges that address transition and change, student development, managing expectations, coaching and communication, and partnership-building with college officials. In these programs facilitated by student affairs professionals, parents focus on building effective relationships with their student and the college to support student success in the collegiate experience.

Appendix B
Staff Training Materials

Leslie A. Banahan

Responding to Parent Concerns

* Listening is the most important skill for working effectively with people

* Ask questions

* Confirm understanding of the situation and what you are being asked to do

* Consult and follow policy: be prepared to explain policies from an educational/student development perspective

* Refer carefully and appropriately

* Assure parents that you are available; offer name, phone number, or e-mail address

* Follow up to see that the situation has been resolved

* Know your professional limits; understand your personal limits

* Know when it's time to refer to your supervisor

Tips for Working With Unhappy Parents

* Stay calm

* Allow parents to climb "Mad Mountain" (allow parents to tell their story)

* Listen before responding

* Remember, it's not personal (but it can feel that way)

* Strive to understand the emotion behind the words

* Speak positively and choose words carefully

* Acknowledge parents' frustrations ("I'm so sorry this has been such a difficult/frustrating experience for you/your student.")

* Focus on solutions and the future, not blame and the past

* Solve problems WITH students, not for students (avoid parents' attempts to substitute their advocacy for their student's appropriate role in the situation)

* Follow up; provide contact information

* Take the challenge: provide extraordinary, surprisingly great service

Crisis Response to Parents

* Parents will remember (maybe forever) how you react/manage a student crisis

* Understand your role both internally and externally (For example: Will you be talking with the media? Will you be part of any campus judicial discussions or hearings? Will you be speaking with law enforcement officers?)

* Provide information—only say what you know (which may be very little); make no assumptions

* Provide emotional support; remain calm— rehearse the words (never easy to deliver bad news)

* Provide logistical support if parents come to campus

* Serve as campus liaison for parents; assist in communicating with faculty, police, residence hall staff, registrar, bursar, etc.

* Remember, in a crisis, parents may need someone to listen to them and someone to blame for what has happened to their student. Often, student affairs professionals are called upon to meet both needs.

Appendix C
Examples of Parent Orientation Program Activities

Jeanine A. Ward-Roof

Arizona State University located in Tempe, Arizona—57,000 undergraduates

Parent Orientation at Arizona State University includes a program on campus resources delivered by student orientation leaders, a program on student development and the parent experience presented by the professional staff from the Parents Programs Office, meetings with college advisors separately from the students to learn about academic expectations, and a session with a college professor who offers tips for success on campus with the students.

Armstrong Atlantic State University located in Savannah, Georgia—6,900 undergraduates

At the point where the parents and students are separated in the Armstrong Atlantic State University orientation, the program is entitled the Symbolic Cutting of the Cord. While the students are elsewhere on campus the parents have a chance to experience 14 different programs ranging from discussions about the new chapter in their lives, to health issues, the University's vision for the future, and financial aid.

Central Washington University located in Ellensburg, Washington—8,000 undergraduates

Parent orientation includes transitional programs entitled Parents in Transition and Parenting during the College Years. Both of the programs offer parents information on the transitions they and their son or daughter will experience, questions and answers about campus resources, and a reception at the president's house.

Clemson University located in Clemson, South Carolina—13,000 undergraduates

Careers and Fears is a popular program among parents at Clemson University. Through a series of staged phone calls and expert advice, the parents are guided through a typical semester of college. The issues addressed are study habits, time management, health and nutrition, money management, relationships, and accessing campus resources. The program ends by assuring the parents that they have done a great job raising their son or daughter and that their son or daughter will still listen to them even if they are miles away. The program facilitators encourage the parents to establish or revisit current communication patterns and create or reinforce expectations (and consequences when they are not upheld) for their son or daughter while they are on campus. In addition, the university has an extremely active Parents' Council that assists with many activities for incoming and current students. The Council members write letters to all of the incoming freshmen describing the successes and challenges their son or daughter has had, assist with the orientation program by serving on a parent panel where parents can ask any type of question, host Family Weekend events, and create quarterly newsletters.

College of the Holy Cross located in Worcester, Massachusetts—2,700 undergraduates

Parent orientation includes programs entitled Parents as Partners, Community 101, and Alcohol 101. Parents as Partners and Community 101 both share elements of personal stories and focus on educating parents about the unique mission of the College of the Holy Cross. The Alcohol 101 program is described as a disturbingly honest review of survey results on alcohol and drug use on campus. The parents leave this session shocked but state that they appreciate the candor and open discussion about how they can become involved and make a different with these issues.

Florida Atlantic University located in Boca Raton, Florida—18,000 undergraduates

Parent Orientation includes a program entitled Parents' as Partners, an in depth discussion of policies and procedures that offers ways for parents to partner with the university to promote their son's or daughter's success. The Office of Retention also takes this program further and continues to communicate with the parents through a Parents as Partners listserv. This listserv gives the parents greater accessibility to university resources and issues.

Mary Baldwin College located in Staunton, Virginia—800 undergraduates

This all-female institution offers a parent orientation session during move-in weekend. The parents can attend all of the events during the day until 7:30 p.m. when there is a scheduled hugs/kisses, goodbye time. During the day the parents can meet faculty advisors, have dinner, and meet the president. The orientation professional is considering starting a book club for the parents who attend future orientations.

Notre Dame De Namur University located in Belmont, California—1,207 undergraduates

Parent orientation includes a dean's presentation where each of the four colleges' deans provides an overview of his/her college. At the end of the session the parents are divided into groups by their student's major and attend a question-and-answer session with the appropriate dean. Another program that is offered during parent orientation is the Personal Services Session. This session focuses on receiving information from counseling services, public safety, disability services, and health and wellness services. Each of the office representatives offers a brief presentation and then answers questions from the parents.

Texas A & M University located in College Station, Texas—36,000 undergraduates

Texas A & M's parent orientation includes a College 101 session which reviews expectations and registration information as well as university expectations and rules and regulations. In addition, the Partners in Success program, offered by the Department of Student Life, addresses challenges first-year students encounter and how the university and families can prepare for and overcome them.

University of Central Florida located in Orlando, Florida—42,000 undergraduates

The parent program at the University of Central Florida offers a letting-go program facilitated by the Division of Student Development and Enrollment Services. The staff members in these areas have experience dealing with parents and college students making a transition to college. The program is developed to support the parents as their son or daughter begins their transition to college.

University of Connecticut (UConn) located in Storrs, Connecticut—14,000 undergraduates

Parent orientation at the University of Connecticut includes the option to attend several different workshops or mini-tours. The first workshop and tour includes How UConn Can Help My New Student Succeed; residential life and campus safety; and tours of the library, Center for Undergraduate Education, information technologies engineering building, chemistry building, greenhouses, the Jorgan Center for the Performing Arts, and the Asian-American Cultural Center. Mini-tour two includes visiting the UCONN bookstore, Gampel Pavilion (Basketball arena), sample residence hall rooms, student recreation facility, and the Husky Heritage Sports Museum. The Walk-A-Holics tour is a 3-mile walk around the agricultural areas of campus where the participants can visit the horse, sheep, and cow barns and the Dairy Bar for UConn ice cream.

University of Idaho located in Moscow, Idaho—10,565 undergraduates

The campus orientation program is offered to parents with a focus on the involvement opportunities on campus, such as Greek life and residence halls. Breakout sessions include information on these and other activities, as well as transition issues. The program also offers lunch for the parents with the college president, provost and associate deans of the colleges.

University of Missouri–Columbia located in Columbia, Missouri—22,000 undergraduates

This institution hosts a Living On Campus presentation that includes campus dining services, residential life, and Greek Life. They also offer the Professors Perspective, a presentation by a university professor on what students need to do to be successful. Topics include study skills, building relationships, time management, and extracurricular activities.

University of North Dakota located in Grand Forks, North Dakota—13,000 undergraduates

Parent orientation at University of North Dakota includes a 4-hour presentation on the second day of orientation that includes introductions to the family association and their activities, opportunities to network among families and learn about current trends of today's families, and focus on the parent-vs-coach paradigm.

University of Rochester located in Rochester, New York—3,600 undergraduates

A program that is included in the orientation program at the University of Rochester is a session entitled Parenting Your College Student which focuses on communication issues and is sponsored by the dean of students and University Health Service. Another program includes a glimpse of a model class that is taught by university faculty.

University of Texas at Arlington located in Arlington, Texas—18,870 undergraduates

The parent orientation program offers parents a session on FERPA so that they can better understand the law, focus groups where they can provide immediate feedback to the institution about their experiences thus far, and the "hippest parent" contest where parents can enjoy a lighthearted event while their students are registering for classes.

University of Texas at Kingsville located in Kingsville, Texas—5,000 undergraduates

The parents of incoming students are invited to a matriculation ceremony that ends with dinner with the college deans, faculty, and staff. The staff reports that the parents appreciate their inclusion in this event.

Appendix D
Parent Orientation Schedule from Clemson University

Jeanine A. Ward-Roof

Author's Note: Clemson University is a 4-year residential institution located in the southeastern portion of the United States. There are approximately 13,000 undergraduates enrolled on campus and approximately 17,000 total students. The parents and student go through different facets of orientation together and separately as noted in the program schedule. Each year the program serves between 3,600 and 3,900 parents.

Parent Orientation Schedule
Day One – Freshmen

7:30 – 9:45 a.m. .... Check-in
Students and parents

> Enjoy coffee and donuts. Check-in for Orientation, check-in for orientation housing, visit the services fair where your son or daughter can have their yearbook or ID picture taken and you can visit with representative from food service, Academic Support Center, telecommunications, Army and Air Force ROTC's, student organizations, University bookstore, Parents' Council, athletes, alumni, campus ministers, student government micro fridge and lofts, Student Financial Education Service, and local merchants.

8:00 – 8:30 a.m. .... **Introduction to Intercultural Services**
Students and parents

> This is a special meeting for minority students and their parents to learn more about the Educational Support Team (EST mentoring program).

8:45 – 9:45 a.m. .... **Calhoun Honors College Meeting**
Students and parents

> This is a special meeting for students and their parents who have been accepted for membership in the Calhoun College Honors College.

8:45 – 9:45 a.m. .... **Athletic Student Meeting**
Students and parents

> This is a special meeting for students and their parents who have been actively recruited by the Clemson athletic department.

10:15 – 11:30 a.m. .... **Opening Session**
Students and parents

> This program includes a welcome from the orientation leaders, the President and Dean of Students; unique aspects of campus life including traditions and expectations; overview of the schedule; comprehensive student services video; and a panel consisting of representatives from the Career Center, Health Center, Housing Office, Academic Support Center and the Orientation program.

11:30 a.m. – 12:30 p.m. .... Parent Lunch
Parents alone

> Parents enjoy an informal lunch at the football stadium in the President's box.

12:45 – 1:15 p.m. .... Career and Fears
Parents alone

> This program includes the addressing of transition issues students may face while in college. The experts from the counseling and psychological services office, academic support center, career center and dean of students office address the issues that arise in the staged phone calls by orientation leaders. The session ends with the opportunity for parents to ask questions about all of these issues.

1:30 p.m. .... Academic College Meetings
Students and parents begin process but separation varies by college.

> Students and parents listen to the Provost explain academic expectations and then are escorted to various campus locations to learn more about specific college and major academic expectations as well as how to schedule for classes and what requirements need to be satisfied during the first semester of enrollment.

4:30 – 5:30 p.m. .... Laptop Program
Students and parents

> This program addresses technology issues for students.

5:30 – 7:15 p.m. .... Dinner
Students and parents

7:30 – 9:00 p.m. .... Student Life Presentation
Students and parents

> Session includes a lively introduction to campus traditions and a fast-paced video highlighting campus activities. A panel consisting of representatives from the alumni center, university union, athletes, intercultural center, campus recreation, police department and student government offers the participants a plethora of information as well as opportunities to get their questions answered. The program concludes with a skit-format presentation of issues the orientation leaders think the students and parents need to understand and a chance for the orientation leaders to tell the parents and students things they wished they had know prior to their enrollment.

9:00 – 10:30 p.m. .... Parent Panel and Reception
Parents only

> The members of the Parents' Council (current parents of Clemson students) along with two student orientation leaders, the Dean of Students, and representatives from the University bookstore and food service answer questions for parents while relaying information about their campus area, experience or the experiences of their sons or daughters.

Parent Orientation Schedule
Day Two–Freshmen

7:00 – 8:30 a.m. .... Breakfast
Students and parents

8:30 – 10:00 a.m. .... Closing Session
Students and parents

> Session includes information about Air Force and Army ROTC, financial aid, parking, student fees, and ID services. The program concludes by inviting everyone to proceed to a reception at another location where representatives from most offices and departments on campus are waiting to answer their questions. The reception ends with the selection of winners for the parent prizes including campus t-shirts, mugs, and other paraphernalia and football tickets.

9:45 – 11:15 a.m. and 11:45 – 1:00 p.m. .... Housing Showrooms
Students and parents

10:00 –11:00 a.m. .... Greek 101 for Parents
Parents only

> Session includes the opportunity to find out more about campus fraternities and sororities.

10:00 – Noon .... Health Center Tours
Students and parents

10:00 – 11:00 a.m. .... Performing Arts Center Tours
Students and parents

10:30 a.m. – 12:30 p.m. .... Study Abroad Reception
Students and parents

11:30 a.m. – 12:00 p.m. and 12:30 p.m. – 1:00 p.m. .... Being Safe in the Clemson Community
Students and parents

11:00 a.m. – 12:30 p.m. .... Career Center Open House
Students and parents

Appendix E
Home for the Holidays

Leslie A. Banahan

[First printed in *Parents Press,* a newsletter for members of the Ole Miss Parents' Association, The University of Mississippi, W. Smith. (Ed.), Winter 1998.]

As the end of the first semester approaches, students and parents anticipate the long holiday vacation. Both are excited about the holiday visit; both have clear pictures in their minds of what the visit will be like. Unfortunately, these expectations are usually not the same! Changes have been taking place across the miles—at home and at college.

The first extended visit home from college highlights a relationship in transition as students move from adolescence to adulthood. It's sometimes small comfort that the first visit is the most intense; subsequent visits are easier for everyone. Students expect everything at home to be the same, exactly the same. If parents have been bold enough to make some changes in the home or daily family routine, college freshmen may be critical, hurt, and resentful. "How dare they change anything? I'm the one who is supposed to change, not home!" Students often express surprise that life has gone on without them, as if they haven't even been missed.

Parents, on the other hand, are often dismayed at the changes in their students. After all, they have only been in college four months. Unless students have gotten tattoos, a pierced body part or two, or a totally new hair color, they probably look the same on the outside. But, freshmen have been struggling with and finally embracing new-found freedoms. Their schedules are unique to campus life; sleeping on and off during the day, going out around 10 or 10:30 in the evening. Students may flaunt their new adult behaviors to their families, whether the behaviors be culinary ("I would never eat anything that has once breathed on its own"); philosophical ("The meaning of life can't be found in the pursuit of wealth in this capitalistic society"); religious ("I know we've always gone to THAT church, but I've found true inner peace in THIS church"); or political ("Our family may have always voted Democratic/Republican, but we were wrong. I'm vice president of the campus Young Democrats/ Republicans now"). As a survivor of a college freshman's first holiday visit, my advice to parents is to breathe deeply and laugh often! This, too, will pass.

When I ask freshmen to describe the perfect home holiday visit, they describe an extended stay at an expensive resort: luxurious private room and bath, favorite foods available with little or no notice, free laundry service, plenty of time to connect with high school friends, generous entertainment allowance, and well, you get the idea. Rarely do they mention quality time with family, visits with relatives, opportunities to share household chores, or even searching for the perfect summer job. On the other hand, parents look forward to getting the opportunity to talk with their students, to learn the details of their life at college. Parents expect to know where their students are going, who they're going with, and when they will be home. Parents might even think their students will be present for meals, visits with relatives, and anything else that the family might do. Clearly, the situation calls for communication and negotiation.

I advise students to be considerate of their parents and to take into account how much their parents are interested in their lives at college. Home is not a residence hall, and students shouldn't expect to come and go as if they were living with 400 other freshmen. Parents and students need to pick their battles carefully and try to be flexible in negotiating their wants and needs. Communication is the key. As long as everyone is talking and listening, there is no reason that satisfactory compromises can't be reached. And, remember, the first visit is the hardest!

Happy Holidays!